SH*T FOR BRAINS

SH*T FOR BRAINS

TRIVIA YOU CAN'T UNKNOW

HAREBRAINED, INC.

A TarcherPerigee Book

tarcherperigee

An imprint of Penguin Random House LLC
penguinrandomhouse.com

TarcherPerigee with tp colophon is a registered trademark of Penguin Random House LLC.

Most TarcherPerigee books are available at special quantity discounts for bulk purchase for sales
promotions, premiums, fund-raising, and educational needs. Special books or book excerpts also can
be created to fit specific needs. For details, write: SpecialMarkets@penguinrandomhouse.com.

Library of Congress Cataloging-in-Publication Data
Names: Harebrained, Inc. (Firm), author.
Title: Sh*t for brains: trivia you can't unknow / Harebrained, Inc.
Other titles: Shit for brains
Description: [New York]: TarcherPerigee, an imprint of Penguin Random House LLC, [2022]
Identifiers: LCCN 2022003624 (print) | LCCN 2022003625 (ebook) |
ISBN 9780593538296 (trade paperback) | ISBN 9780593538302 (epub)
Subjects: LCSH: Curiosities and wonders.
Classification: LCC AG244 .H35 2022 (print) | LCC AG244 (ebook) |
DDC 031.02—dc23/eng/20220520
LC record available at https://lccn.loc.gov/2022003624
LC ebook record available at https://lccn.loc.gov/2022003625

Printed in the United States of America
1st Printing

Book design by Laura K. Corless

CONTENTS

SH*T FOR BRAINS

INTRODUCTION

When the night starts to wind down, and you or one of your friends drops a "You know what? We should . . ." the idea is usually toast by morning. While we never got around to the cross-country RV trip or starting that podcast, that wasn't the case with *Sh*t for Brains*. The trivia we grew up with was stale, safe, and unrelatable, and we knew we weren't alone in wanting something different. Our tireless enthusiasm for the very weirdest minutiae carried it all the way from a puny spreadsheet to this very book. This volume is, at its core, the product of longtime friends nerding out about things they love.

Every rabbit hole we went down led us to things we didn't even know we were looking for, and we hope what we've put together gets you lost in some of your own. Across these twelve chapters, *Sh*t for Brains* brings the *how*s and the *why*s to bits of trivia we've always taken for granted, like stripping a fact about an ancient Egyptian royal custom down to its nuts and bolts: a teenage king trying to piss off his dad. Looking for the bigger human truths in these stories led us to the biggest truth of all: Our world is, always was, and always will be, a flawed, funny, farty place.

BAD
COMPANY

MOUTHING OFF

During World War I, the United States Radium Corporation employed women to paint glow-in-the-dark dials with radioactive paint, instructing them to shape the brushes with their lips and fingers. Once women's jaws started to erode from radiation poisoning, the company covered it up by alleging that the workers were afflicted with syphilis.

COCK ROCK

After record label DGC wanted to censor the nude baby on the cover of Nirvana's 1991 album *Nevermind*, the band suggested covering the offending image with a sticker that said, "If you're offended by this, you must be a closet pedophile."

UNDERWATER ON THEIR CABLE BILLS

In the wake of 2008's Hurricane Ike, Comcast continued to bill South Texas residents for "unreturned equipment," despite that very equipment being destroyed by the hurricane.

SWINDLER'S LIST

Author and Holocaust survivor Elie Wiesel lost millions from both his personal fortune and his foundation to late Ponzi schemer Bernie Madoff.

NOT DOWN TO CLOWN

After getting orders from their parent company, Disney, Hollywood Records didn't just stop production on Insane Clown Posse's 1997 breakthrough horrorcore album *The Great Milenko*, but actually recalled the 100,000 copies that had already shipped, claiming that the material didn't "fit the Disney image." This for sure had nothing at all to do with the Southern Baptist Convention's call for a boycott of all things Disney after the parks started hosting "Gay Days."

SAUCY LINK

In 2015, Heinz unknowingly allowed a QR code on their ketchup bottles to direct to an expired URL, which by then was home to a porn site.

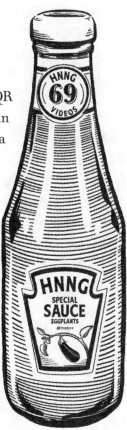

FROM ONE LOSER TO ANOTHER

After a trader known as the London Whale lost JPMorgan Chase 6 billion dollars in a 2012 trading scandal, CEO Jamie Dimon received a pep talk phone call from NFL star Tom Brady. I'm sure the pep talk helped when Dimon found out that his annual bonus was cut in half to a measly $10.5 million.

WE DEPRECIATE YOUR BUSINESS

In case you ever think that you're bad with money, just remember that Rupert Murdoch's News Corporation bought Myspace for $580 million in 2005, only to sell it six years later for $35 million.

JINGLES ALL THE WAY

In 2009, the ABC network cut over two minutes from *A Charlie Brown Christmas*, a beloved TV special that warns against the commercialization of the holiday, in order to give more airtime to commercials.

YACHT ROCKED

During the 1983 Sydney to Hobart Yacht Race, Rupert Murdoch's boat rammed into a boat sponsored by rival media mogul Ted Turner only ten kilometers from the finish line, sinking it, so that he was unable to complete the race. Turner followed up by challenging Murdoch to a fistfight.

KIDDIE COCKTAIL

Applebee's has gotten in trouble a few times for serving underage patrons, like the time they served a Long Island iced tea to a five-year-old New Yorker, a margarita to a California toddler, and a spiked apple juice to a Detroit fifteen-month-old.

4 OUT OF 5 RACISTS RECOMMEND

In 1985, Colgate acquired a company that offered a toothpaste called Darkie to many Asian countries. If the name wasn't suspect enough, Darkie's logo was an Al Jolson–esque performer in black-face. It took executives until 1989 to change the name of the product to Darlie and update the packaging, although the Chinese name of the brand still translates to "black person toothpaste."

DYING FOR A SMOKE

Marlboro Red cigarettes earned the nickname Cowboy Killers after five of the seven Marlboro Men died of smoking-related illnesses.

CHALLENGE ACCEPTED

Introduced in 1969, Nerf balls were marketed as "the first indoor ball" and had the extremely catchy and not at all buzzkilling slogan "You can't hurt babies or old people."

YOU'VE COME A WRONG WAY, BABY

BMW was forced to recall their female-voiced navigation system in the '90s after a bunch of German men complained that they wouldn't take directions from a "woman."

DID NAZI THAT COMING

In 2016, Microsoft introduced an AI chatbot to Twitter with the hopes of helping it improve its language skill. After less than twenty-four hours in Twitter's toxic mire, the bot was tweeting things like "I fucking hate feminists" and "Hitler was right." Unsurprisingly, the project was promptly canceled.

ALMOST LOST THE PHARMA

Insufferable Pharma Bro Martin Shkreli started his first hedge fund in 2006 and after just a year lost a $2.3 million lawsuit to Lehman Brothers. They failed to collect before going bankrupt in 2008.

FATHER SOLD SEPARATELY

Barbie needed a friend, so Mattel introduced Midge in 1963. She landed with a thud, and was soon pulled off the shelves. She appeared back on the scene in the 1980s, fully pregnant, as part of the Happy Family line. Poor Midge couldn't catch a break, as some retailers refused to carry her because she was packaged separately from the baby's father.

I THINK WE'RE GETTING ZIPPED OFF

In 2007, the leading zipper brand YKK was fined 150 million euros for running four zipper price-fixing cartels.

FAST FOOD, SLOW PEOPLE

Because Americans suck at math and think that a third is less than a quarter, A&W's Third Pounder was unable to compete with McDonald's Quarter Pounder and was dropped from the menu.

BLOWING SMOKE

Philip Morris published a report in 2001 saying that they saved the Czech government money because smokers often die before retiring. They then sued the Uruguayan government after it passed anti-smoking legislation, claiming that the restrictions would cause irreparable damage to the brand.

BLOOD MONEY

From the late 1970s to 1985, Bayer sold contaminated blood products to hospitals, causing twenty thousand people to contract HIV. After they found out, they pulled the products off the US and European shelves but continued to sell them in Asian and Latin American countries.

REICH FATHER, REICH SONS

Best known for their massive influence on American conservative politics, the Koch brothers inherited much of their initial wealth from their father, who helped establish oil refineries for the Nazis in the lead-up to World War II.

COLA WARS

In 1990, PepsiCo briefly had the sixth-largest navy in the world after trading their products with the USSR for vodka and a small fleet of warships.

COMPACT, YET WOMBY

In 2001, Honda was about to release a car called the Fitta (its tagline was "Small on the outside, big on the inside"), when it realized that *fitta* was a vulgar Swedish term for *vagina*.

NEW AND UNPROVED

Cigarette company Philip Morris discovered the fire-safe cigarettes they introduced in 2002 were actually much more likely to cause fires. They responded by firing the scientist who ran the risk analysis testing.

BET YOUR BOTTOM DOLLAR

In 1974, the owner of FedEx gambled the company's last $5,000 on blackjack and managed to save the company from bankruptcy.

FLYING THEIR FREAK FLAGS

All of the American flags at Disney's Magic Kingdom are missing a stripe or star so that they don't have to be taken down at night or in bad weather.

SKRILLA IN MANILA

In 1993, Pepsi ran a contest in the Philippines giving the lucky person who found the number 349 under their Pepsi cap one million pesos ($40,000). They accidentally printed 800,000 winning caps, which led to riots, firebombs, and at least five deaths.

TRUMPED-UP KICKS

Skechers Shape Ups shoes claimed that they would help people lose weight and tone their butt muscles without having to go to a gym. They even had a real live chiropractor endorse them! Unfortunately, after it was discovered that the chiropractor was married to a Skechers marketing executive, the shoe company had to pay a $40 million class action lawsuit.

CHILI CON CARNAGE

In 2004, the Mexican restaurant chain Chi-Chi's decided to close all their locations and file for bankruptcy after four customers died and another 660 fell ill from a Hepatitis A outbreak.

GET RICH OR LIE TRYING

After Coca-Cola was sued by a consumer protection agency for overstating the health benefits of Vitaminwater, they defended themselves with the argument that "no consumer could reasonably be misled into thinking Vitaminwater was a healthy beverage."

DON'T MESS WITH TAXES

With businesses eager to take advantage of the state's tax loopholes, there is a drab, two-story building in Delaware that serves as the legal address to more than 285,000 US companies, including Coca-Cola, American Airlines, JPMorgan Chase, Ford, Apple, Google, and Walmart, to name a few.

ICE ICE MAYBE

Ice cream company Breyers changed some of their recipes in the mid-2000s and included so many additives that they can no longer be labeled "ice cream" in the US and Canada.

AN OFFER THEY SHOULDN'T REFUSE

In 2000, Netflix's founders were laughed out of Blockbuster's headquarters when they offered to sell the company for $50 million. Ten years later, Blockbuster filed for bankruptcy.

SMOKE SCREEN

The Type A/B Personality Theory was invented by the cigarette industry in the 1950s to prove that coronary heart disease and cancer were symptoms of high-stress personality types rather than tobacco use.

MINIMUM RAGE

For several months in 2013, one perk of working at McDonald's was access to a website that offered advice on how to stretch your paycheck with recommendations like: breaking food into smaller pieces to feel full, returning holiday gifts for cash, and getting a second job. The McResources website also suggested, "Stop complaining, as stress hormones rise by 15% after ten minutes of complaining."

SEEING THE LIGHT

The inventor of Keurig K-Cups regretted all the environmental waste from his invention so much that he left Keurig and started a solar panel company.

TROUBLE BREWING

There are two beer companies called Budweiser—one in America and another in the Czech Republic. They have been fighting over the name since 1907.

NOW WITH EXTRA POISON

In 1952, Kent cigarettes introduced a filter made from the latest cutting-edge technology: asbestos. You know, that toxic material that causes lung cancer.

INSULT TO INJURY

As automobiles became more popular, there was a huge spike in pedestrian deaths and it outraged the public. The automobile industry successfully shifted the blame to the victims, asserting that they didn't know how to behave in traffic. In fact, the industry coined the term "jaywalking," with "jay" meaning *hick* or *rube*.

CELL SERVICE

All US prison phone service is dominated by two private companies, Global Tel Link and Securus, who make billions of dollars a year. Due to their exclusive contracts, they can now charge inmates and their families $1 a minute, huge "connection" fees, and have lobbied against in-person visitation.

AVOIDING TAXES BY DESIGN

Despite averaging $40 billion in global sales, Ikea is actually a nonprofit company "dedicated to furthering the advancement of architecture and interior design." Not coincidentally, the designation also gives them a 3.5 percent tax rate.

START MAKING CENTS

A bottle of Coke had been five cents since launching in 1886, and after more than seventy years they finally needed to raise the price. Coca-Cola lobbied the US Treasury to mint a 7.5-cent coin, since they felt a dime was too much to charge.

BULLSHIT DETECTOR

Advanced Tactical Security & Communications Ltd, a UK company, sold a fake bomb detector device to twenty countries in the Middle East and Asia for $60,000 apiece. After Iraq spent $78 million on them, it was revealed that the device was nothing more than a dowsing rod and the company owner went to jail for fraud.

CANCER CULTURE

Nonprofit Susan G. Komen for the Cure has sued hundreds of smaller nonprofits for using the words "for the cure" or the color pink.

MANDATORY TRAINING

When 1,300 miners went on strike in 1917, American mining company Phelps Dodge, along with the local sheriff and a two-thousand-strong deputized posse, kidnapped the miners and union organizers at gunpoint, loaded them into train cars, and dropped them two hundred miles away. They also had the town's phone and telegraph lines cut to prevent the story from getting out.

MISS INFORMATION

In 2012, Miss America claimed to make $45 million of scholarship money available to women annually, but in actuality only gave out $500,000.

WHERE THERE'S SMOKE, THEY'RE FIRED

In 1993, *Dateline NBC* strapped model rocket engines to GM trucks so the trucks would explode on impact for a televised crash test. After GM sued, three producers were fired.

I FIND YOUR LACK OF FAITH DISTURBING

20th Century–Fox had so little confidence in *Star Wars* that they traded away all movie licensing and merchandising rights to director George Lucas in exchange for his $500,000 directorial payment. The deal made Lucas a billionaire.

WURST NAME EVER

Despite its name, the American fast-food chain Der Wiener-schnitzel is about as authentically German as its food. They serve hot dogs and burgers, the masculine *der* is incorrect, and a missing space suggests that the food is made from people from Vienna.

THIS STINKS

Axe Body Spray marketed their product to horny, insecure young men, and it worked so well that they became the number one men's deodorant brand. The company took a step back from this approach after their brand gained a reputation as a spray used only by horny, insecure young men.

SACKED

In 2010, Frito-Lay created an environmentally friendly, 100 percent compostable chip bag but had to stop using them after eighteen months because people complained that the bags were too noisy.

FINISHING MOVE

After being outed as gay in one of their stories, PayPal co-founder Peter Thiel funded Hulk Hogan's lawsuit against Gawker Media, which ultimately bankrupted it.

SEEPING THROUGH THE CRACKS

America's love affair with Procter & Gamble's fat substitute Olestra came to an abrupt end in the late '90s after it was found to cause anal leakage.

FUMBLD THE BAG

Social networking site Tumblr was bought by Yahoo! for $1.1 billion in 2013, banned adult content in 2018, and was sold to the owner of WordPress for $3 million in 2019.

SUPPLY ON THE SIDE ECONOMICS

Engineer John Delorean helped develop some all-time classic American cars, including Pontiac's GTO and Grand Prix, and eventually went out on his own to work on his passion project: the Delorean, aka the bitchingest car in the *Back to the Future* cinematic universe. His new venture wasn't working out financially, though, and he resorted to some drastic measures to keep it funded. He was later arrested and charged with conspiracy to obtain and distribute fifty-five pounds of cocaine, valued at $24 million.

SEE WHAT CONDITION MY ROAST CHICKEN IS IN

Singer Kenny Rogers started a restaurant chain in 1991 called Kenny Rogers Roasters and went on an episode of *Late Night with Conan O'Brien* to promote it. On the episode, Kenny failed a blind taste test, choosing chicken from the NBC cafeteria rather than his own. A year later Kenny Rogers Roasters filed for bankruptcy.

YOU GOTTA FIGHT FOR YOUR RIGHT TO POULTRY

Before he became a beloved and enduring fast-food mascot, "Colonel" Harland Sanders tanked his law career by getting in a courthouse fistfight with his own client and wounded a rival business owner in a shootout.

RUNS INTO TROUBLE

In 2021, NBC originally planned to air a new competition TV series called *Ultimate Slip 'N Slide* after the Tokyo Olympics, but the project was flushed after a giardia outbreak gave upward of forty crew members explosive diarrhea.

BODILY
FUNCTIONS

MERRY CRASSMAS

In Spain's Catalonia region, nativity scenes include a very special character: El Caganer, a villager taking a dump in the corner. Traditionally, the figure was a male peasant with a red hat; nowadays the mad crapper can be anyone, including politicians, movie stars, and video game characters.

SUCK OF THE IRISH

In ancient Ireland, subjects showed ultimate submission to their king by sucking his nipples.

UNDERARM HER

The pheromones in a man's armpit sweat can help a woman relax and even boost her mood. It is most effective when applied to the lips. One hundred percent of scientists do not suggest doing this without prior consent.

PRE-LEWD

Mozart put the "assical" in *classical* by naming one of his canons *"Leck mich im Arsch,"* which translates to "Lick Me in the Ass."

WOMB SERVICE

Capitalizing on US women's limited access to birth control, Lysol marketed itself as a douche and a contraceptive from the 1920s through the 1950s.

MINOR SURGERY

Believing that their pain receptors weren't yet fully developed, doctors often operated on newborns sans anesthesia. The practice was formally put in time-out in 1987.

DOCTOR'S ODORS

Believing that fighting one noxious vapor with another was the key to health, doctors during London's 1660 plague outbreak recommended that patients fart into a jar and keep it on hand to inhale in case of exposure.

GOT TO-GO CUP

Think twice about pouring yourself a cup of the brown stuff. A 1997 University of Arizona study found that 20 percent of office mugs carry some degree of fecal matter.

PUBLIC CERVIX ANNOUNCEMENT

In 1946, Disney produced an animated educational short called *The Story of Menstruation*, and it's believed to be the first time the word *vagina* was used on film.

STINKY BUNS

Rúgbrauð, an Icelandic rye bread, is nicknamed þrumari or thunder-bread because it's legendary for creating powerful farts. It's not alone in this gassy world; pumper-nickel is a German rye bread whose name translates to "the devil's fart."

TOOT!

CUTTING-EDGE TECH

First called a flexible saw, the chain saw was originally used more as a surgical tool than for cutting wood or slashing teenagers.

IT'S IN THE CAN

Released in 1960, Alfred Hitchcock's *Psycho* was the first American film not just to show a toilet, but to feature an audible flush.

IF YOUR ERECTION LASTS MORE THAN 3,000 YEARS, CONSULT A DOCTOR

Egypt's teenage King Tut was mummified with a fully erect penis in tribute to Osiris, the god of rebirth. This act had the added value of pissing off his dad, a big advocate for monotheism.

NUTTIN' TO SNEEZE AT

In 1624, Pope Urban VIII forbade Catholics from using snuff, a powdered form of tobacco. Snuff had a tendency to cause sneezing, which was just a smidge too close to sexual ecstasy for him.

I'LL DRINK TO THAT

A cholera outbreak in 1854 London was traced to a leaky cesspool. The only people in the area not afflicted with Ye Olde Loose Bowels? Area monks and brewery workers, as both groups consumed more beer than water.

DYNABITE

In nineteenth-century Pennsylvania, a dentist began chronicling a nightmarish condition: exploding teeth. As it turned out, if two different metals had been used to fill the teeth, then the whole mouth would be turned into an electrochemical cell . . . aka a low-voltage battery.

HAPPY ACCIDENT

Alchemist Hennig Brand thought that he could distill gold from urine. After stockpiling and boiling 1,500 gallons of pee into a thick syrup, he failed to discover any gold. But by isolating a waxy substance from the final product, he inadvertently gave us an easy process for harvesting phosphorus.

TOY CHEST

Skipper, Barbie's little sister, was introduced in 1964. About ten years later she had a major growth spurt when Growing Up Skipper came on the scene. The doll's breasts would grow as you turned her arm.

REFINED SUGAR

In Tudor-era England, sugar was new on the scene and very expensive. Those who could afford it often had black teeth from overconsumption, leading some to blacken their teeth to give the illusion of wealth.

OLD WIVES' FAILS

There were a lot of crazy old-timey "cures" for menopause, some of those being: ingesting arsenic, taking mustard baths, attaching leeches to the cervix, shock therapy, and playing golf.

OVARY AND OVARY AGAIN

The average menstruating person has 425 to 475 periods throughout their lifetime. Added up, this equates to around ten years (that's 3,500 days!) of cramping, bloating, bleeding, and high potato chip intake.

THAT'S A SHIT-TON

Did you know that a "buttload" is an actual measurement? If someone has a buttload of diarrhea, that means they're holding back approximately 126 gallons of poo.

THEY REALLY DO HAVE A WORD FOR EVERYTHING

The German word for a lower back tattoo (aka tramp stamp) is *arschgeweih.* Translation: ass antlers.

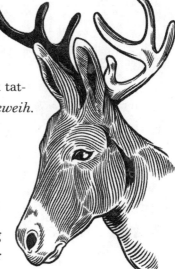

WASTE OF SPACE

Astronauts poop by taping a bag over their butts. To lighten their load, they leave the bags behind, and as of 2021, there were ninety-six bags of human waste on the moon's surface.

PYRAMID SCHEME

Up through the seventeenth century, Western Europeans used ground-up mummies as everything from a general cure-all to an aphrodisiac. This practice is thanks to a misinterpretation of the Arabic word *mumyia*, a petroleum resin from West Asia.

POTTY MOUTH

Ancient Romans used human urine as a mouthwash and antiseptic. The practice was so popular that it was often sourced from other countries, with Emperor Nero even establishing an import tax.

GREATEST SHITS

In 2004, a Dave Matthews Band tour bus emptied its septic tank from a Chicago bridge. Passengers on the boat tour passing directly below got a front-row seat to the carnage. All eight hundred pounds of it.

THE SHOW MUST BLOW ON

Featured at the 1900 World's Fair in Paris, Joseph Pujol's act consisted of celebrity impressions, trick cigarette smoking, and playing a variety of musical instruments . . . all done via a hose inserted in his anus. Pujol could break wind on command,

and went by the stage name Le Pétomane (translation: *Fartomaniac*). The fartiste had previously appeared at the Moulin Rouge, and was even captured on silent (but deadly) film by none other than Thomas Edison.

SURVIVAL RATE: SKIM TO NONE

Dissatisfied with the results from attempted blood transfusions, North American doctors in the 1840s attempted the procedure with milk as a blood substitute.

FOR THE GOOD OF THE HOLE

Ancient Romans used a communal rag on a stick for wiping after a poo. This is rumored to be the origin of the expression "getting the shit end of the stick."

SLASHING THE BUDGET

The human skeletons used in many of your favorite horror movies are the real deal, but not for extra spookage. A realistic fake is often way too expensive.

BEAUTY TIPS

The epidermal growth factor facial costs more than $600 and uses a collagen-rich serum made from cells cloned from the discarded foreskins from human infant penises.

YANKEE TOOTLE

When he wasn't busy inventing bifocals and openly cheating on his wife, Benjamin Franklin found time to write an essay called "Fart Proudly."

IT'S A FRUIT, NOT A NUT

In 500 BCE, Aztecs discovered a fruit with an ugly exterior, roundish shape, and purported aphrodisiac qualities. They christened it the āhuacat—*testicle*. We know it as the avocado.

DON'T SLEEP ON THEM

If someone you know is immune to contagious yawning, keep an eye on them! It can indicate everything from selfishness to full psychopathy.

GONE APPETIT

Coprophagia is the super fancy scientific word for eating poo.

HOLEY SITE

Saint Fiacre, a seventh-century Irish monk, is said to have cured his inflamed poop chute by sitting on a rock and praying. Thanks to this miracle, he is now the patron saint of hemorrhoids. Legend has it that the imprint of his hemorrhoids remain on the stone to this day, and anyone who sits on the rock will be cured.

ASTRONOMICAL PROPORTIONS

Before Sally Ride's groundbreaking weeklong trip to space, her male colleagues at NASA designed her a space-proof makeup kit and suggested that she bring a hundred tampons. You know, just in case.

ALL THE BUZZ

Let's Trim Our Hair in Accordance with the Socialist Lifestyle was a 2004 North Korean propaganda TV special urging citizens to keep their hair short, citing "evidence" that long hair could deprive nutrients from the rest of the body.

BREAKING THE SOUND BARRIER

The 1974 film *Blazing Saddles* by proto–dad joker Mel Brooks was the first to feature an audible fart.

LIFEGUARD ON DOODY

Are your eyes red and itchy after a dip in the pool? Don't blame the chlorine! It's more likely a cocktail of feces, urine, and dirt.

PLAYER TYPE TWO

Bayer developed the DIDGET blood glucose meter to sync with the Nintendo DS so diabetic nerds could be rewarded with points and access to games for checking their blood sugar.

iPATCH

In 2012, biohackers developed a substance called Ce6 that gave people the ability to see in the dark when injected into the eye. Creep tested, creep approved!

SNOOZE CONTROL

It's impossible to sneeze or hiccup in your sleep, because when you sleep, so do the required reflexes. Unfortunately, this does not apply to farts.

STARTING FROM THE BOTTOM

The anus is the first part of the human body to develop in the womb.

FORKED UP

Upper and lower teeth in humans used to sit right on top of each other, like a little guillotine for your food. The introduction of utensils like chopsticks and forks gave us the slight overbite we have today.

PUT SOME PEP IN YOUR STEP

Putting a chili pepper in your socks is a practice recommended anywhere from sixteenth-century Japan to modern doomsday prepper messageboards. Why? The capsaicin in chili peppers is an irritant not just to the mouth, but to all parts of human skin, and can create a feeling of warmth.

NO PRINT, NO STINT

Chemotherapy drug Capecitabine can cause a temporary loss of one's fingerprints.

IT'S ALL ON YOUR HEAD

Redheads are genetically predisposed to be less responsive to anesthesia and more sensitive to heat and cold.

MAKING THE CUT

A castrato is a male singer who has had his testicles removed to maintain his higher, prepubescent vocal range. The practice was first documented in the ninth century, but it really gained steam in sixteenth-century Italy.

CREEPSAKE

Frankenstein author Mary Shelley carried around her late husband's heart until her death years later. Due to a bout with tuberculosis, it had calcified and survived his cremation.

PUFF, PUFF, ASS

Inspired by American First Nations tradition, seventeenth-century London doctors used tobacco smoke enemas to treat patients for everything from stomachaches to near-drownings. In fact, blowing smoke up someone's butt was such a well-regarded practice for resuscitating drowning victims that smoke enema kits were installed at various points along the River Thames.

STAY POSITIVE

In 2016, a doctor injected himself with Charlie Sheen's blood in an attempt to prove that his alternative treatments had cured the actor of HIV. They hadn't.

FLUSHIN' REVOLUTION

Russian Secret Service documents reveal that Stalin had special toilets installed to collect the poop of other foreign leaders. The samples were then sent to a secret lab where they were analyzed in an attempt to get some psychological insights into his political rivals. For instance, little or no potassium could indicate a nervous disposition.

WAIST BANNED

After its establishment in 1934, the Motion Picture Production Code (aka the Hays Code), banned filmmakers from showing a woman's belly button on-screen. To skirt the rule, on-screen showgirls would wear jewels in their navels.

DIRTY DICK-TATOR

The leader of communist China from 1949 to 1976, Chairman Mao Zedong refused to wash his genitals, stating that he'd rather "bathe [himself] in the bodies of [his] women."

DONGGONIT

Thanks to rumors that tainted pork could cause their genitals to shrink and retract, men in 1967 Singapore were gripped by a great penis panic. Hospitals were flooded and pork sales shriveled.

DON'T HAVE A COW, MAN

Its name is straight out of cattle country, but a bite from the lone star tick can cause a lifelong allergy to red meat.

MATH WHIZ

MIT's Walker Memorial building has chalkboards installed over its urinals (sorry, STEM gals!) so that male students can formulate while they urinate.

CONSOLE-ATION PRIZE

Paging Dr. Mario! "Nintendo Thumb" is a real medical condition involving stress injuries from excessive gaming.

PEARLY YELLOWS

In 2013, scientists were able to grow teeth from a specific type of stem cell found in urine.

GETTING BUFF

The word *gymnasium* comes from ancient Greece, and roughly translates to "exercise naked."

TOUGH TITTIES

Amazon is an ancient Greek word that means "without a breast." It refers to the mythological group of badass women warriors who cut off their right breasts to enhance their archery skills.

TAKES GUTS

In 1961, Leonid Rogozov was the only doctor at a remote station in Antarctica and was forced to perform an emergency appendectomy on himself.

DICK MOVE

Swaffelen was the Netherlands word of the year in 2008. It means to repeatedly smack one's penis against something or someone. The term gained popularity after a Dutch student was arrested for swaffeling the Taj Mahal and the video of his subsequent arrest went viral.

MIDSIZE DOESN'T MATTER

In 2011, the world's most confident man had the word *mini* tattooed on his penis in order to win a Mini Cooper.

THE ORIGINAL RUSSIAN NESTING DOLL

A Russian peasant named Valentina Vassilyeva holds the world record for giving birth to the most children: sixty-nine. She's on record as giving birth twenty-seven times, with each birth producing multiple children: sixteen pairs of twins, seven sets of triplets, and four sets of quadruplets. Her husband Feodor always wanted a big family, so he went on to have an additional eighteen children with his second wife.

DOESN'T MAKE SCENTS

A gene mutation found most often in Southeast Asian populations, and almost all Koreans, changes the composition of sweat so that it does not produce BO.

GOOD TO THE LAST PLOP

Black Ivory Coffee is the world's rarest and most expensive. It's known for its exceptionally smooth taste, achieved by passing the beans through an elephant's digestive system and picking them out of the dung just prior to brewing. Drink up!

LAP-OR-TOOTLE

The word *feisty* was once interchangeable with *farty*. For example, a small feisty dog that sat on an old lady's lap could be blamed for any farts that might arise.

SAY YOUR PRAYERS

The origins of saying "God bless you" after someone sneezes can be traced back to the plague of 590 CE. Pope Gregory I declared that nonstop prayer was essential for divine intervention. Since sneezing was often the first sign that someone was sick with the plague, the pope ordered everyone to say "God bless you" after an "achoo."

#2 ON THE BESTSELLER LIST

There is a Japanese cultural phenomenon known as "Mariko Aoki." Named for the woman who first brought it to national attention, it refers to the sudden urge to defecate upon entering a bookstore.

TESTE SUBJECTS

For almost two decades in the early 1900s, John Brinkley made millions of dollars by transplanting goat testicles into men's scrotums with the promise of enhanced virility. Unfortunately, forty-two of these men died from postsurgical infections, which makes sense because he never had any formal medical training, and any credentials he did have were bought from diploma mills.

BUTTON FLY 'TIL I DIE

The most common source of penile injuries are zippers. Every year about 1,700 men head to the ER for zipping their tip.

CELEBRITY
SLIGHTINGS

CASHLESS TRANSACTION

A year after Johnny Cash's death, "Ring of Fire" cowriter Merle Kilgore licensed the song to a hemorrhoid cream commercial. The other writer on the song, June Carter Cash, was quick to stop the project before it got off the ground.

PADDING THEIR RÉSUMÉ

In 1985, a young Courteney Cox starred in a tampon commercial and made history by being the first person to ever say the word *period* on US television.

RUNG HIS BELL

Law & Order's Richard Belzer once had his own talk show, and had Hulk Hogan on to promote the first WrestleMania. He asked Hulk to demonstrate some wrestling moves, resulting in Belzer getting choked out and splitting his head open on the ground, and then suing the Hulkster for $5 million.

ACTING OUT

By the age of twenty-one, Mark Wahlberg had committed dozens of offenses, several of them hate crimes. These included chasing and throwing rocks at Black schoolchildren and assaulting two Vietnamese men.

FROM GYRO TO HERO

Britney Spears's little sister and former Nickelodeon star Jamie Lynn Spears once broke up a fight at a Hammond, Louisiana, Pita Pit restaurant by jumping behind the counter, grabbing a long bread knife, and waving it around.

DON'T SLEEP ON THIS GUY

Since 1967, Harvard's Hasty Pudding Theatricals Society has issued a Man of the Year award to a famous entertainer. The 1969 winner suggested changing the name to the Nice Guy as Far as We Know award. Excellent idea, Bill Cosby!

COCK BLOCKED

Not wanting to condone eating meat, dedicated vegetarian Paul McCartney refused to let "Weird Al" Yankovic record a parody song called "Chicken Pot Pie" (to the tune of "Live and Let Die").

FIGHTING WORDS

Infinity-hyphenate 50 Cent questioned boxer Floyd Mayweather's literacy by challenging the boxer to read an entire page of a Harry Potter book out loud without error. If he was successful, 50 Cent would donate $750,000 to a charity of Mayweather's choosing. Mayweather declined to participate.

GET YOU A WOMAN WHO CAN DO BOTH

Golden Age actress Hedy Lamarr was also an inventor who created the Frequency Hopping System (the basis for cell phone technology) for the Allies in WWII and was the first woman to perform an orgasm on-screen in a non-pornographic film.

WHEN PIGS FLY

Pink Floyd was doing a photo shoot for their iconic album *Animals* when their forty-foot helium pig balloon became untethered and forced Heathrow Airport to shut down all flights.

A BLESSING AND A CURSE

Samuel L. Jackson started using his signature word, *motherfucker*, to overcome a lifelong stuttering problem.

SMELL YOU LATER

Leslie Nielsen, star of the Naked Gun films, loved pranking people with a fart machine so much that his tombstone reads "Let 'er Rip."

GENETIC MATERIAL GIRL

Madonna has her own personal sterilization team who are tasked with removing her DNA from all performance venues.

NO SMALL PARTS

If you look closely, you can see porn star Ron Jeremy in the background of *The Godfather Part III* in the role he was born to play: "Man Chewing Toothpick in Crowd."

WE WERE ON A BREAK POINT

Mulleted tennis hunk Andre Agassi was so jealous of his then-girlfriend Brooke Shields kissing Joey on the TV show *Friends* that he smashed his Wimbledon trophy.

CRASH AND LEARN

Oscar-nominated actor Gary Busey was staunchly against helmet laws until his 1988 motorcycle accident in which he fractured his skull and suffered permanent brain damage.

PET SOUNDS

Freddie Mercury had planned to record a series of duets with Michael Jackson, but called it quits after one recording session because he was too creeped out by having to work next to MJ's pet llama.

STAYIN' ALIVE

Bee Gees member Robin Gibb narrowly survived a deadly 1967 train accident that killed forty-nine people.

LAME EXCUSE

Kanye West has had a lot of cringeworthy moments in the public eye, but none more so than when he stopped a concert performance because he wanted the whole audience to stand before he started his next song. One fan remained seated, and West announced that "this is the longest I've had to wait to do a song, it's unbelievable." It was later brought to his attention that the fan was in a wheelchair.

PURPLE-HEADED MONSTER

David Joyner, the actor who played Barney the dinosaur in the '90s, became a tantric sex expert and "unblocks the energy" of two to four "goddesses" a week.

HONKY GORY

Fabio murdered a goose with his beautiful face while he was on the inaugural run of a new roller coaster at Busch Gardens theme park in 1999.

DOUCHES ARE WILD

Ben Affleck was banned from the Las Vegas Hard Rock Hotel and Casino in 2014 after he was caught counting cards in a high-limit blackjack game.

MAUL MY CHILDREN

Both '60s actress Tippi Hedren and her daughter, Melanie Griffith, appeared in the 1981 film *Roar*. The movie featured dozens of untrained big cats and of the 140 crew members, more than half of them suffered dire injuries ranging from puncture wounds to broken bones. Fourteen-year-old Griffith suffered a scratch on her face so deep it required plastic surgery.

THUGGISH RUGGISH BLOKE

After featuring in their 2003 song "Home," as well as appearing in its video, singer and drummer Phil Collins was made an honorary member of hip-hop group Bone Thugs-N-Harmony; the group christened him "Chrome Bone."

WRITE WHAT YOU KNOW

A TV personality wrote a 1998 novel about a tall, bitter, sexually predatory newsman who gets forced out of his job and starts murdering his former colleagues. That TV personality was Bill O'Reilly.

HE TOUCHED A LOT OF KIDS

McFeely sounds like the code name for sex act performed at a burger joint, not the middle name of Fred Rogers, aka the host of *Mr. Rogers' Neighborhood*.

BLAST RITES

Johnny Depp paid $3 million to shoot Hunter S. Thompson's ashes out of a cannon.

ODOR EATER

Steve Jobs thought his all-fruit diet eliminated the need to shower, earning him the lonely night shift during his time at Atari.

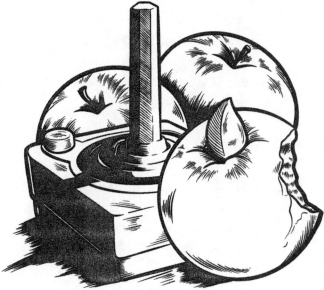

REEL TOO REAL

Martha Stewart once dated Anthony Hopkins in the early '90s, but broke it off because she was unable to separate him from the psychopath that he played in *Silence of the Lambs*.

DIDDLE ME THIS

Stars of the 1960s *Batman* TV series, Adam West (Batman) and Frank Gorshin (The Riddler), were invited to an orgy but eventually kicked out for refusing to break from their characters.

TOXIC ROCK SYNDROME

Qualified actress and unqualified wellness guru Gwyneth Paltrow sells a lot of products that go up your vagina on her website GOOP. Most notably, jade eggs that are part of a (likely made-up) ancient Chinese practice that is supposed to increase vaginal muscle tone, hormonal balance, and "feminine energy."

NANNER BANNER

Musican Jack White turned red with anger when the University of Oklahoma's school paper published his tour rider, which included the following request: "this is a NO BANANA TOUR (seriously). We don't want to see any bananas in the building."

AN OFF-RAMP HE COULDN'T REFUSE

In the immediate aftermath of 9/11, Michael Jackson, Elizabeth Taylor, and Marlon Brando fled New York City on a cross-country road trip together. Apparently Marlon Brando annoyed his two companions by insisting they stop at nearly every Burger King and KFC they passed.

REVENGE OF THE NERD

Bill Nye the Science Guy had to get a restraining order against his ex-wife after she was caught pouring herbicide on his prized rose bushes.

HAPPY DAYS

California native Pat Morita, best known for playing Mr. Miyagi, spent the bulk of his childhood in a hospital with spinal tuberculosis, enduring almost a decade of surgeries and physical therapy. In 1943 he was "released" to the internment camp where his family was detained.

WHY DON'T YOU HAVE A SEAT OVER THERE

Chris Hansen, host of the controversial show *To Catch a Predator*, was caught cheating on his wife by hidden cameras arranged by the *National Enquirer*.

CHART UNTOPPER

Before she was a huge '80s pop star, Cyndi Lauper was working as a stripper under the name Carrot to save up money for some music equipment. Her strip club boss didn't think she could sing and told her to stick to stripping.

STRINGS ATTACHED

Actress Candice Bergen grew up with a famous ventriloquist dad who might have preferred the dummy to his daughter. The first clue was when he gave the dummy a bigger bedroom than her. The second might have been when he left her out of his will and left $10,000 to the puppet.

WALKEN ON THE WILDSIDE

Oscar-winning actor and subject of endless bad impressions, Christopher Walken worked as a teenage lion tamer, was on board Robert Wagner's boat when Natalie Wood mysteriously drowned, and made an appearance in Madonna's controversial coffee table book, *SEX*.

RIFF-OFF ARTISTS

In the late '60s, a group of Texas muscians pretended to be the British band the Zombies and toured the US to sold-out shows. They later formed a real band, calling themselves ZZ Top.

MAKE LOATHE TO THE CAMERA

Don't try to snap a candid photo of actor Sean Penn. He shot at people in a helicopter who were trying to film his 1985 wedding, dangled a photographer over a ninth-floor hotel balcony in 1986, and punched a movie extra who tried to take a photo of him in 1987.

COME WITH ME IF YOU DON'T WANT TO LIVE

Executives at Orion Pictures wanted O. J. Simpson to star as the Terminator, but James Cameron didn't think he would be "believable" as a killer.

WORTH A SHOT

Elvis Presley once wrote a letter to President Nixon denouncing the Beatles, hippies, drugs, and communism. He then asked for a federal agent's badge that he thought would allow him to carry a gun anywhere in the world.

IN-FLIGHT ENTERTAINMENT

Candid Camera host Allen Funt was on a 1969 flight to Florida where hijackers demanded to be taken to Cuba. Other passengers had recognized Funt and assumed the whole thing was a stunt for his show, and ignored his pleas to take the situation seriously. They were finally convinced when the plane touched down in Cuba.

ONLY THE GOOD DIE YOUNG

In 1970, Billy Joel tried to kill himself by swallowing a handful of barbiturates with furniture polish. Obviously it didn't take, and he turned his suicide note into the song "Tomorrow Is Today."

BREAKING CHARACTER

While serving as Sean Connery's personal martial arts trainer on the Bond film *Never Say Never Again*, Steven Seagal got pissed off when the actor attempted to outmaneuver him during a session and broke Connery's wrist.

RANK AND VILE

Gun fanatic and Tea Partying rock 'n' roller Ted Nugent admitted to have dodged serving in Vietnam by not bathing for a month, vomiting on himself, and shitting his pants.

ROUGH RIDER

Late rapper DMX was arrested for impersonating a federal agent to gain access to a gated area at an airport. When the attendant refused to let him pass, he crashed his SUV through the gate. He then tried to get away by hijacking a car, telling the driver he was an FBI agent.

OH, YOU NASTY BOYS

Satirical newspaper *The Onion* was almost sued out of business by a certain R&B icon because of an article titled "Dying Boy Gets Wish: To Pork Janet Jackson."

BLIND FAITH

Possibly it was all the drugs, his emotional state, or just gullibility, but one day Eric Clapton got a cold call from a witch who told him how to get his wife back: take herbal baths, smear his blood on a crucifix, and chant midnight incantations. When that didn't work, she told him to fly to the US and have sex with a virgin (her); she then stalked him and then sent pregnant photos of herself to the tabloids. The jig was up when it was discovered that she had a pillow stuffed under her dress.

DESSERTERS WILL BE SHOT DOWN

Holders of the Carvel's "Black Card" get seventy-five years of free ice cream at any Carvel location. Lindsay Lohan had hers revoked within six months of being issued after her family abused it with excessively large and frequent ice cream orders.

ONE WIFE, TWO WIFE, DEAD WIFE, NEW WIFE

Dr. Seuss had an affair while his wife was suffering from cancer and depression. A few months after his wife killed herself, he married his mistress.

THE NUTTING PROFESSOR

Eddie Murphy denied being the father of Scary Spice's (Mel B) child until a paternity test proved otherwise.

FIXER UPPERS

Fake TV psychatrist Phil McGraw, aka Dr. Phil, has been accused by past guests with substance abuse issues of providing them with drugs and alcohol right before tapings.

PHOTOSHOOT

On December 8, 1980, the last known photo of a living John Lennon was taken. He was with Mark David Chapman, a Lennon superfan and also his assassin.

WEENYBOPPER

In 2013, 1960s pop star Chubby Checker sued Hewlett-Packard for using his name without permission on an app that claimed to measure the size of a person's penis. Considering the $.99 app was downloaded a grand total of eighty-four times, the half billion dollars that he was seeking makes it seem like Ol' Chubs was overcompensating for some-thing.

SMASH BROS

Gallagher, the watermelon-smashing comedian, gave his younger brother permission to use his act in the early '90s, but ten years later sued him to stop performing his hacky act.

HOW FAR HE'S FALLEN

In 2009, Coolio performed at a UK university and dove off the stage into the arms of . . . no one. When he crashed into the floor, the students immediately stole his shoes and jewelry.

FEMME FATALE

Before she was a TV sex therapist, Dr. Ruth was a scout and sniper for Haganah, an underground Jewish military organization.

CRAZY PLANE

In 1982, Ozzy Osbourne's guitarist Randy Rhoads died while joyriding in a stolen airplane that crashed when he tried to "buzz" the band's tour bus.

DIAMOND IN THE ROUGH

The late Dustin Diamond (aka Screech from *Saved by the Bell*) leaked his own sex tape in 2006 and spent three months in jail after stabbing someone in a Wisconsin bar in 2014.

WHO RUM THE WORLD

In 2001, rapper Da Brat was given probation for hitting a woman with a rum bottle. Six years later she was sent to prison for *doing the exact same thing*.

BARK IN BUSINESS

EGOT winner and best-selling female music artist of all time Barbra Streisand has two clones of her deceased pet dog Miss Samantha. Their names are Miss Scarlet and Miss Violet, and Barbra often takes them to visit the grave of their "mother."

4

CRIME
&
DEATH

GOING ELECTRIC

Between 1753 and 1786, more than a hundred French bell ringers were electrocuted due to the belief that the sound of ringing bells could disperse thunder and lighting.

SHOOT FOR THE STARS

John Hinckley was so obsessed with actress Jodie Foster that he moved to Connecticut to stalk her while she studied at Yale. After failing to get her attention, he resolved that the only way she would notice him was if he assassinated then-president Jimmy Carter. Before he could get to Carter, Reagan was elected and the rest was history.

TRAGIC KINGDOM

In 1968, two young boys playing in an abandoned New York City building found the body of thirty-one-year-old Bobby Driscoll surrounded by religious pamphlets and empty bottles. His body was unclaimed and he was buried in a pauper's grave. About two years later, his mother tracked him down after reaching out to his former employer: Walt Disney Studios. Before dying from drug abuse–related issues, Driscoll had been in their stable of child stars, appearing in some wildly popular films and even voicing Peter Pan.

WALK OFF

HBO sitcom *Curb Your Enthusiasm* accidentally did a pretty, pretty, pretty good thing and helped clear a man of murder charges. Outtakes from an episode confirmed his alibi that he was at a Dodgers game at the time of the murder.

TORCHDOWN

Late TLC singer and rapper Lisa "Left Eye" Lopes accidentally burned down the house of her boyfriend, NFL player Andre Rison, while attempting to burn his sneaker collection in one of the home's bathrooms.

BUTCHERING A NAME

Joseph-Ignace Guillotin was a 1700s French physician and activist who was looking for a way to make executions more humane and less of a public spectacle. While he did not invent it, his family was so embarrassed to have the guillotine named after them that when the French government refused to rename the death machine, they changed their family name.

DOES KIDS, PARTIES

When he wasn't busy murdering teenage boys and young men, serial killer John Wayne Gacy was very active in his suburban Chicago community, even appearing at events as Pogo the Clown.

BYE-BYE BABY

The term *autoinfanticide* means to "go back in time and kill oneself as a baby." No one has yet to accomplish this (that we know of).

RUN FOR YOUR LIFE

Treadmills have existed for thousands of years, and in 1818 they were rebranded as a torture device. Per the UK's Prison Act of 1865, all male prisoners were subject to as much as three months of walking or climbing to nowhere. They have since evolved into popular exercise machines and laundry racks.

LITTERED WITH BODIES

Genghis Khan's reign was responsible for so many deaths that the earth's carbon dioxide levels dropped by an estimated 700 million tons during his time in power.

PARA-NOID

In 1989, a Georgia man named Kenneth Noid held two Domino's employees hostage, believing that the chain's "Avoid the Noid" campaign featuring an animated pizza-sabotaging villain of the same name was a personal attack. He demanded $100,000 and a getaway limo. Despite neither being delivered in thirty minutes or less, the hostages were released unharmed.

GUN SHOW

Charles J. Guiteau assassinated twentieth US president James Garfield over an imagined slight, and he chose an ivory-handled gun because he thought (no, he *knew*) it would look dope as hell in a museum.

TURNS OUT, IT DOESN'T GIVE YOU WINGS

Fitness model Greg Plitt was struck and killed by a commuter train. It was, in fact, the very train he was attempting to outrun as part of an energy drink commercial he was self-producing.

CULT CLASSIC

Cleveland's finest industrial export, Nine Inch Nails, recorded their smash-hit 1994 album *The Downward Spiral* in Los Angeles at 10050 Cielo Drive. The private residence was notable for its lush grounds, hillside location, and for the being the site where the Manson family murdered actress Sharon Tate and four of her friends.

REGRETS, I'VE HAD A FEW

Talk about Must See TV! Singer Nancy Sinatra skipped a visit to her father, Frank, so she could watch the series finale of *Seinfeld*. About fifteen minutes into the show, he suffered a heart attack and died later that night.

ONE-STOP SHOP

Your middle school bully's favorite store, Abercrombie & Fitch, opened in 1892 as an outfitter for wealthy outdoorsmen, aka your great-great-grandparents' middle school bullies. In fact, Abercrombie is where Ernest Hemingway purchased the duck-hunting rifle he later used in his suicide.

COME HEIL OR HIGH WATER

As part of the Nazi plan to occupy Russia, Hitler wanted to kill all residents of Moscow and turn the city into a lake.

WHAT A TOOL, MAN

Before he made it big as a TV family man, Tim Allen was arrested in 1978 at a Michigan airport with more than one pound of cocaine. Facing life in prison, he was sentenced to only two years thanks to a classic legal maneuver: ratting out your friends.

THEIR FIRST ANGEL

The founder of Victoria's Secret sold the business for one million dollars in 1982, and after eleven years of poor investments, he died by suicide after jumping from the Golden Gate Bridge. At the time of his death, Victoria's Secret was worth one billion dollars.

SAVE MONEY, LIVE LESS

In 2011, a South Carolina man fatally stabbed his wife inside of a Walmart. Instead of closing, the store had employees rope off the bloody crime scene so customers could still enjoy their low, low prices.

BLADES OF GORY

The last time a person went head-to-head with a French guillotine was in 1977. The device was officially retired in 1981 when France abolished the death penalty.

THAT BLOWS

In 1979, a woman attempted suicide by jumping from the eighty-sixth floor of the Empire State Building, only to have a gust of wind blow her back on to the eighty-fifth floor.

GAUDY BODIES

Mount Everest boasts the world's most macabre lost and found: an area named Rainbow Valley, so called for the colorful jackets, gear, and corpses of failed climbers littering the hillside.

A SHORT CUT TO FAME

On June 23, 1993, Lorena Bobbitt carved herself into the public eye when, after being raped by her abusive husband, she cut off his penis and threw it into a field. The penis was found and reattached to John Wayne Bobbitt, who went on to form a band called the Severed Parts and star in two pornos, while Lorena endured years of media ridicule.

HAVING THE NEIGHBORS FOR DINNER

Archaelogical evidence shows that the first round of British settlers at Jamestown resorted to cannibalism to survive "The Starving Time," the brutal winter of 1609 where an estimated 75 percent of their population was lost to starvation.

I WANT YOU FOR YOUR BODY

In 2015, Charles Manson called off his upcoming jailhouse wedding after learning that his much younger fiancée was hoping to one day display his corpse for profit.

LIFE IMITATING ART

Edgar Allan Poe's only novel, *The Narrative of Arthur Gordon Pym of Nantucket*, features a cabin boy named Richard Parker who is cannibalized by crew members after a shipwreck. Fifty-one years after the book was written, an actual cabin boy named Richard Parker suffered the exact same fate.

STIFFED

Silent film star Charlie Chaplin's body was stolen and held for a £400,000 ransom. The plan was foiled when his widow refused to pay, and the body was found eleven weeks later.

DOUBLE TROUBLE

Translating to "substitute criminal," *ding zui* is the Chinese term for hiring a body double to stand trial and serve a sentence in your place. It is rumored to be fairly common practice among China's most wealthy, and has been keeping facial recognition experts in business since the late 1950s.

BUSINESS IS DEAD

Due to the spike in murders related to cocaine trafficking in 1980s Miami, the Dade County Medical Examiner's office rented a refrigerated trailer from Burger King to store corpses.

SO I HIRED AN AXE MURDERER

Frank Lloyd Wright built the Wisconsin estate Taliesin as a love nest for him and his mistress. Just prior to a luncheon, the chef suffered a psychotic break and set fire to the building, going after the guests with an axe as they attempted to flee the building. A total of seven people died. The chef never gave a motive, starving himself to death shortly after the massacre.

STICKING IT UP TO THE MAN

Depression-era outlaw Pretty Boy Floyd was known to destroy mortgage documents during his bank robberies, making him a folk hero to many struggling Americans. He was even memorialized in song by Woody Guthrie.

FOOTLOOSEN RESTRICTIONS

For sixty-seven years, dancing anywhere but an approved venue was illegal in Japan. Even then, the festivities had to stop at midnight. The ban was lifted in 2015, and clubs could even apply for twenty-four-hour licenses.

Thanks to their tubular shape and malleability, hot dogs are the number one choking hazard for kids three and under.

MANSPREADING

Peter the Great had his wife's lover drawn and quartered, then preserved the lover's head in a jar full of alcohol as a memento.

DIDN'T WORK OUT THE BUGS

In an attempt to protect China's rice crops, Chairman Mao ordered a mass killing of sparrows. Since sparrows ate grain *and* bugs, this led to an unchecked population growth of locusts, which ruined harvests and caused a deadly famine that killed millions.

RAISE THE ROOF

The Copsey brothers built a one-room stone jailhouse in the mining boomtown of Lower Lake, California, the town's first. The project was finished in 1876, and the brothers went out to celebrate. They raged so hard that they were arrested and became the jail's first occupants. They were also the first to escape when they remembered they not yet finished attaching the roof.

GANG WEARFARE

In early 1900s America, straw hats were all the rage during the summer—both for men and women. Traditionally, one would switch to a felt hat on September 15, and those who did not were faced with everything from public ridicule to a visit from the fashion police (gangs of teenagers who would grab your straw hat and stomp it to death in front of you). The hat bashers once decided to get an early start, and on September 13, 1922, an eight-day riot ensued, with a mob of about a thousand ruthlessly destroying straw hats all over New York City.

SATURDAY IN THE MORGUE

Terry Kath, a founding member of dad rock band Chicago, died in 1978 while playing around with a gun he believed to be unloaded. He told his friend, "Don't worry about it . . . look, the clip's not even in it," before fatally pulling the trigger.

GATED COMMUNITY

As a condition of his surrender, drug lord Pablo Escobar was allowed by Medellín police to design his own prison. He called it La Catedral, and it featured a soccer field, waterfall, bar, and even a luxury dollhouse for visits from his daughter. Escobar escaped after a year and a half, and the property is now a public meditation space run by Benedictine monks.

ONE-HIT WONDER

Despite marrying his thirteen-year-old cousin, decades of drug and alcohol abuse, a history of violent outbursts, and two of his wives meeting mysterious and untimely ends, singer Jerry Lee Lewis was arrested only once, in 1976, for drunkenly brandishing a gun in front of Elvis Presley's Graceland estate.

THAT'S LOW, MEIN

In 2002, a Chinese snack shop poisoned the food of a rival business, killing forty-nine people in the process.

TALLY WACKER

Ancient Egypt's King Merneptah defeated Libyan forces in the early 1200s, and as a final brutal act he had his soldiers collect the penises from the nearly thirteen thousand Libyans killed in battle.

SHOW YOUR WORK

The first person to jump off the Brooklyn Bridge was Robert Odlum, a professional high diver who wanted to show that people don't die from simply falling through the air. He proved this theory to be correct when he fell 135 feet safely through the air, only dying when he hit the water.

MURDER SHE WROTE, MURDER HE DID

When iconic true crime author Ann Rule began writing about Ted Bundy's murders, she was unknowingly working directly next to him at a suicide prevention hotline.

HEALTH NUTS

In 1984, the first and largest to date bioterror attack in US history was perpetrated by an Oregon cult that contaminated salad bars with salmonella, infecting 751 people. They were hoping to incapacitate the locals so that the cult-approved candidates would win local elections.

CLOTHES MINDED

Even though it hadn't been enforced in a very long time, in 2013 France revoked a 214-year-old law that said it was illegal for women to wear pants.

DEATH IS FOR THE BIRDS

For reasons both practical and spiritual, Tibetans often have "sky burials" in which they carry corpses up to the mountains and leave them to the elements, including vultures.

ARCADIC LAWS

With leaders believing it was a gateway to a life of crime, pinball was banned in New York City public spaces in 1942, with many other major cities following suit. By the 1970s, the restrictions had loosened only for pinball machines to be replaced with more compact and easier to maintain video games.

GOING UNDER COVERS

Bob Lambert is a former undercover officer for the British police who was forced to resign after it was revealed that he was carrying on sexual relationships with women in the activist groups he was infiltrating. One of the women, with whom he had a child, was awarded almost $700,000 in damages after learning his true identity.

KEEP CALM & THROW THEM IN A CARRY-ON

In 2015, Singapore Airlines introduced seventeen-hour nonstop flights and added a special cupboard on their A340 aircrafts for discreetly holding a corpse in the event of a passenger's death.

OLD FAMILY RECIPE

Nannie Doss was an American serial killer who murdered eleven people between 1927 and 1954, mostly by poisoning; police apprehended her shortly after the autopsy of her fifth husband revealed high levels of arsenic in his system. The press had a field day with the story, giving her sensational nicknames like the Giggling Granny, Arsenic Annie, and the Jolly Black Widow.

BOOKING IT

Serial killer Ted Bundy acted as his own lawyer during his 1977 hearing, and after being granted a visit to the courthouse law library to research the case, he managed to escape through a window.

NO REFUND-AMENTALISTS

The terrorists behind the 1993 World Trade Center bombing were caught after trying to get the $400 deposit back on the rental van that was destroyed in the blast.

CRASS TRANSIT

Before the 2003 updates to the NYC transit system, attendants would sprinkle chili powder into the turnstile token slots to keep people from sucking out the tokens and reselling them.

SHORT STAFFED

The producers of *Willy Wonka & the Chocolate Factory*, which was filmed in West Germany, had a hard time finding enough little people for the cast because the Nazis had killed so many of them.

SOME LIGHT THERAPY

Be it placebo effect or truly calming properties, Scotland and Japan have seen a drop in both crime and suicide after installing blue streetlights.

CHEEKY LAD

In late-seventeenth-century London, there was a sexual attacker named Whipping Tom, who would slap women's buttocks in public and shout "Spanko!" before running away. The attacks were so frequent that women took to carrying knives or scissors and men trolled alleyways dressed as women in hopes of catching him in the act.

ROMAN CANDLES

It's rumored that the Roman Emperor Nero lit Christians on fire to illuminate his garden at night.

POWER HUNGRY

In 1672, an angry Dutch mob shot, mutilated, and strung up their prime minister, Johan de Witt, and then cannibalized his corpse.

NAMING PLIGHTS

The English town of Shitterton got so tired of people stealing their welcome sign that they eventually replaced it with a 1.5-ton stone.

CRIMINAL OPERATIONS

Dr. Leo Stanley was the resident MD at San Quentin prison from 1913 to 1951. During his tenure, he committed atrocities ranging from coerced sterilizations to testicle transplants.

EYE-Q

Dr. Thomas Stoltz Harvey famously removed Albert Einstein's brain during an illegal autopsy. He also removed his eyes, and gave them to the late physicist's eye doctor. To this day, the pair remains in a New York safe-deposit box.

IN THE NAME OF THE LAW

In 2012, former Colorado sheriff Patrick J. Sullivan Jr. was arrested and charged for trading meth to male addicts in exchange for sex. The best part of this story is that he was booked at his namesake facility, the Patrick J. Sullivan Jr. Detention Center.

ASHES TO ASHES, PUFF TO PUFF

Members of the hip-hop group Outlawz confirmed during a 2011 interview that they smoked the ashes of Tupac Shakur.

SOAKS TO BE YOU

You'd think that whatever ended the life of the second person to survive going down Niagara Falls in a barrel would have to be incredibly epic. Instead, circus performer Bobby Leach slipped on an orange peel, got an infection, and died in 1926 from complications from the subsequent amputation.

DRUGS, MAN

SOBERING THOUGHT

In Russia, there is a treatment for addiction called the Dovzhenko Method, aka Coding, in which a therapist uses hypnosis and placebo doses to convince patients that a code has been put in the brain that will kill them if they go back to their substance of choice.

BEACHED PARTY

The *Mayflower* landed on Plymouth Rock because the Pilgrims on board had run out of beer. At the time, beer was the main source of hydration for people of all ages, as it was safer than water.

DRINK AND DERIVE

A group of drunk Japanese scientists discovered that you can improve a superconductor's conductivity by 62 percent if you soak it in red wine.

PROPAGANJA

Until the late 1910s, pot was known mostly by its botanical name: cannabis. Officials introduced *marijuana* into the lexicon to capitalize on anti-immigrant prejudice in states bordering Mexico and its gulf. California's first bill criminalizing cannabis even referred to it as *locoweed*.

END OF DAZE

Author of *Brave New World* and *The Doors of Perception*, Aldous Huxley was a huge fan of LSD, and on his deathbed, requested his wife to shoot him up so he could go on one final trip.

POWDER OF THE INTERNET

Bret Easton Ellis, author of *American Psycho*, made a slight goof on Twitter when he tried to text his drug dealer, but instead asked his 350,000 followers to bring him some cocaine.

FEEL-GOOD HIT

Dopamine is a chemical released in the brain that causes pleasure. Your dopamine levels rise by 50 percent from food, 100 percent from sex, and 250 percent from cocaine.

THERE'S SOMETHING ABOUT MARIJUANA

Cameron Diaz claims to have bought pot from Snoop Dogg while the two were in high school together.

CRACK ROCK THE VOTE

Even after getting caught freebasing crack in a hotel room, Washington, DC mayor Marion Barry was reelected in 1994.

BAT-SHIT CRAZY

In 1938, the US Federal Expert on Marijuana, Dr. James C. Munch, claimed under oath that he had turned into a bat after smoking "two puffs of a marijuana cigarette." He stayed in the position until 1962.

CLEARED OF ANY BONG DOING

In 2003, the DEA targeted actor Tommy Chong of Cheech and Chong fame; he was arrested and sentenced to nine months in jail for financing and promoting his son's bong business. Federal prosecutors admitted to going after Chong because they saw his stoner movies as trivializing the War on Drugs.

CLEGGY DOSES DALLAS

Back in the 1980s, Michael Clegg was a one-man MDMA-moving machine. He named the drug Ecstasy, and at one point this Catholic priest was moving 500,000 pills a month in the Dallas area alone.

TOTAL BODY TRANSFORMATION

Anabolic steroids are a legal drug that can build up muscle mass and reduce fat. They also have side effects like giving men breasts and tiny testicles, women giant clitorises, and everyone male pattern baldness.

IN THE BODY BAG

During Prohibition, the US government poisoned alcohol to thwart bootleggers but ended up killing approximately ten thousand people.

MARKETING OF THE BEASTS

In the early 1980s, Coors Brewing Co. created a werewolf mascot named Beer Wolf to help promote beer sales at Halloween, but later rebanded him a ready-to-party jock who worked as a lifeguard. They eventually killed him off, but there's no word if they used a silver bullet.

CALL OF COOTIE

Cooter "Cootie" Brown was rumored to have lived on the Mason–Dixon line and had family on the North and South. Not wanting to be drafted by either side, he got drunk and stayed drunk for the entire Civil War.

SHOTS FIRED

Hans Island is an uninhabited island near Greenland, with Canada and Denmark both claiming it as a territory. Both countries' militaries periodically visit the island to remove each other's flag and to leave a bottle of booze from their respective country. It's known as the Whisky War.

FRUIT COCKTAIL

Drinkers can reduce the severity of their next hangover by drinking Korean pear juice before consuming alcohol. Studies show that it helps the body metabolize and eliminate alcohol quickly. So remember this new saying: "Pear before beer, you're in the clear. Beer before pear, barf everywhere."

WATER-BASED SOLUTION

Temperance groups helped to popularize drinking fountains in hopes that free and clean drinking water would curb alcohol consumption.

BUT I HAVE A DOCTOR'S NOTE

In 2005, a Frenchman successfully sued pharmaceutical company GlaxoSmithKline for $257,000 after claiming that the drugs he took to treat his Parkinson's disease turned him into a compulsive gambler and self-described "gay sex addict."

FENDER BENDER

Country legend and champion substance abuser George Jones notoriously drove a riding lawnmower eight miles to get to the closest liquor store after his wife hid the keys to all of his cars.

SMUGGLING ACTOR

A pre-fame Bill Murray was arrested in 1970 at Chicago's O'Hare Airport for traveling with ten pounds of marijuana he intended to sell. He was busted only because airport security overheard him making a joke about having a bomb in his bag.

KNOW YOUR AUDIENCE

The rock band Queens of the Stone Age once performed at a rehab clinic but were immediately shut down during their opening song, "Feel Good Hit of the Summer," which solely consists of the lyrics "Nicotine, valium, vicodin, marijuana, ecstasy, and alcohol . . . c-c-c-c-c-cocaine."

SNORT FILMS

When actors snort fake cocaine on camera, the inside of the coke straw is typically coated with petroleum jelly to avoid getting a little sugar in the actors' boogers.

D.I.WINE

During Prohibition, a company called Vine-Glo sold a solid grape juice concentrate with the following warning attached: "After dissolving the brick in a gallon of water, do not place the liquid in a jug away in the cupboard for twenty days, because then it would turn into wine."

ON-SCREEN CHEMISTRY

The producers of TV's *Breaking Bad* hired actual DEA chemists to consult on the script's depiction of meth production, wanting it to be fully accurate.

SEAMENY COCKTAIL

Call it American ingenuity or Americans' willingness to get drunk. During World War II, US Navy members created a drink called Torpedo Juice which was a combination of 180-proof grain alcohol (which also happened to be the fuel used in torpedo motors) and pineapple juice.

TOMB STONED

The oldest stash of cannabis was found in the 2,700-year-old grave of a Chinese shaman.

SECRET TO EXCESS

Scientists have studied Ozzy Osbourne's entire genome in an attempt to understand how he has survived decades of extreme drug abuse.

LSD SOUNDSYSTEM

The Grateful Dead were known to have traveled with their own chemist who supplied them with LSD and doubled as their sound engineer.

EXCHANGE STUDENTS

The very first online transaction was done between Stanford and MIT students selling marijuana.

NUMB & NUMBER

Before novocaine was invented in 1905, cocaine was the primary anesthetic used by dentists to numb gums.

MILITARY GRADE-A SHIT

In an effort to help them stay alert and boost their endurance, Nazi soldiers were given a product called Pilot's Salt or Tank Chocolate—two really fun names for methamphetamines!

PACIFIER

In the nineteenth century, a popular children's medicine called Mrs. Winslow's Soothing Syrup claimed it was "likely to soothe any human or animal," which is absolutely true, as it contained morphine.

OLD STYLE

The oldest surviving beer recipe originates from Mesopotamia and is approximately four thousand years old. It consists of brewing loaves of multigrain bread mixed with honey and dates.

SHIP TON OF WEED

In 1987, a ship carrying twenty-two tons of weed in three-pound coffee cans dumped all of it into the sea as they were being chased by the Brazilian authorities. The cans washed up on Brazil's coastline and the contents were smoked by the locals. It's known as the Summer of the Cans.

TAKE ME TO YOUR DEALER

Famed astronomer Carl Sagan used to write pro-marijuana essays under the pseudonym Mr. X, in which he recounted the ways marijuana inspired his work and enhanced his sensual and intellectual experiences.

THE REICH STUFF

Adolf Hitler got a series of daily injections (sometimes up to twenty a day) which included: caffeine, E. coli, oxycodone, strychnine, crystal meth, and heroin.

HOPPY DAYS ARE HERE AGAIN

The end of Prohibition in America is unofficially celebrated on April 6 as "New Beers Eve."

PRODUCT OF THE SYSTEM

Prison wine, aka pruno, is an alcoholic drink made by prisoners from fruit, candy, and bread. The concoction is usually hidden in walls or toilets while it ferments.

STAND-UP COMIC

In 1951, Disney published a very racist comic in which Mickey Mouse and Goofy are drug dealers who sell a speed-like drug called Peppo to the people of Africa.

DON'T HAVE A MOSCOW

Back in 1634, Russian Czar Alexis created some very strict penalties for smoking tobacco. For your first offense, you got whipped, a slit nose, and transported to Siberia. For your second offense, you were executed.

BIRD'S THE WORD

The term *going cold turkey* gets its name from the opiate withdrawal symptoms of turning pale and getting goose bumps.

WEB-SLINGING DRUGS

Bored with space, NASA started testing the effects of different drugs on a spider's ability to build an effective web. Apart from caffeine, speed, mescaline, marijuana, and sleeping pills, LSD was the only drug that improved the integrity of the web.

CHILD BEERING

For five generations, the family that used to own Budweiser had a stupid tradition: Budweiser beer would be dropped onto their firstborn son's tongue before they could be nursed by their mothers at birth.

LEVERAGE OF CHOICE

During Norway's first aircraft hijacking in 1985, the hijacker drank the plane's entire beer supply, and eventually surrendered his weapon in exchange for more beer.

AMERICAN EXCEPTIONALISM

Champagne can be produced in the USA due to the fact that the US Senate never ratified the Treaty of Versailles.

ZIGGY'S STARDUST

David Bowie and Queen recorded the scat-filled hit "Under Pressure" in a twenty-four-hour session fueled by competing egos, cocaine, and wine.

SMOKING SANCTION

Because they liked their lungs as pure as their bloodline, the Nazis were the first political party of the twentieth century to run a major anti-smoking campaign.

G.I. BRAIN DRAIN JANE

In 2012, paramedics were reportedly called to Demi Moore's house after she lost consciousness from doing too many whip-its.

PLASTERED WALLS

Wat Pa Maha Chedi Kaew is a Buddhist Temple in Thailand that is built from more than 1.5 million Heineken and Chang beer bottles.

FOUR MORE BEERS!

At the inauguration of seventh US president Andrew Jackson in 1829, the twenty thousand attendees got absolutely hammered and trashed the White House.

WAR ON DRUGS

During the Vietnam War, US field troops would consume small amounts of C-4 plastic explosive to get high.

PAID THROUGH THE NOSE

Aerosmith singer Steven Tyler, aka the "Demon of Screamin," claims to have spent over $5 million on cocaine throughout his lifetime.

FIX INCOME

The term "junkie" comes from addicts collecting and selling scrap metal to pay for their heroin in the early 1900s.

WE'RE NOT GONNA TOKE IT

Heavy metal hair band Twisted Sister never drank, did drugs, or partied, but their record label asked them to keep that a secret so it wouldn't hurt their image and sales.

POWERBOMBED

A man of epic proportions and equally epic feats, Andre the Giant once consumed 119 beers in six hours.

BONUS ROUND'S ON ME

Pat Sajak, the host of *Wheel of Fortune*, admitted in 2012 to regularly getting drunk on "two or three or six" margaritas before taping.

EXECUTIVE ORDER

Despite the fact that it takes three weeks for beer to brew and age, FDR received a truckload of ready-to-drink beer from Yuengling on the exact day that Prohibition was repealed.

HIGH & DRY

The word *boofing* has two definitions: the first is a kayaking term for keeping your bow from submerging. The second is a term for consuming drugs or alcohol through the anus.

DR. FEELGOOD

One of the founders of Johns Hopkins Hospital and the doctor who pioneered the use of sterilized medical gloves, Dr. William

Stewart Halsted developed an addiction to cocaine after "testing" it on himself as a local anesthetic.

SIGN OF THE TIMES

The 420 mile marker on I-70 in Colorado was stolen so many times that the state's Department of Transportation replaced it with one that read 419.99.

YOUTH CULTURES

Touted for increasing vitality and sex drive, performance-enhancing supplements made from the dried flesh of dead infants were being smuggled out of China in 2012.

CLEAN BILL OF HELL

If you're going through methadone withdrawal, it's possible you'll experience some of the following side effects: visual hallucinations, extreme paranoia, and spontaneous orgasms.

WHAT A PILL

The man who developed ibuprofen, Stewart Adams, decided to test the drug on himself in 1971 because he was horribly hungover and had to make a speech in a few hours.

CRIPPLING ADDICTION

In the Stephen King novel *Misery*, a writer is held captive by a crazed fan who does horrific damage to his mind and body. The fan represented cocaine, as the book was written at the height of King's addiction.

START A TAB

Twenty years after founding Alcoholics Anonymous, Bill Wilson experimented with LSD and came to believe it could be beneficial to recovering alcoholics.

FIXER DOWNER

Available on drugstore shelves in the 1890s, Bayer marketed heroin as a cough suppressant that could make you feel like a (very sleepy) hero.

HOP PROPERTY

In 1759, Guinness signed a nine-thousand-year lease for the St. James's Gate Brewery.

GOD
DAMN
IT

THE SIN OF PRIDE

Hoping to introduce the king of the jungle to the king of kings, in 2004 a Taiwanese man was mauled by a lion after jumping into a zoo enclosure in an attempt to convert the animals to Christianity.

SOUL FOOD

The Cult of Pythagoras (circa 530 BCE), led by the Greek mathematician, practiced communal living and vegetarianism. Beans were also forbidden over concerns that one's soul might escape via fart.

PRAY FOR OUR TROOPS

During World War II, isolated and preindustrial South Pacific islands were often airdrop sites for American servicemen and their supplies. "Cargo cults" formed after their departure, with the Indigenous people performing rituals that mirrored the soldiers' behavior in hopes that it would draw them (and their items up for trade) back to the island.

BIBLE BELCH

St. John the Baptist church in Chiapas, Mexico, is also known as the "Coca-Cola Church," where churchgoers drink shots of the soda to help release evil spirits through burping.

NOT IN HIS IMAGE

God is the only character on *The Simpsons* to have ten fingers and ten toes.

BLESS THIS MESS

Asher yatzar is an Orthodox Jewish blessing thanking God for good health. It is recited after engaging in the act of defecation or urination.

KEEP THEM OFF THE NAUGHTY LIST

Saint Nicholas (yes, that one) is the patron saint of prostitutes. He learned of a father who lost all his money and had nothing left for his daughters' dowries, putting them at risk of a life of sex work. Not wanting to embarrass the father, St. Nick came to the house at night and anonymously left a bag of gold.

THE HAND OF GOD

Ganglion cysts typically develop on the wrist, and can be popped by hitting them with a thick book. Since the Bible was often the heaviest book most families owned, the cysts were dubbed Bible Bumps.

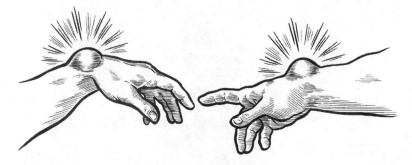

COMEDY ROAST

Christian martyr Saint Lawrence of Rome was sentenced to die by being roasted alive. Legend has it, when he was being burned he told his executioners, "Turn me over, I'm well done on this side." Today he is the patron saint of chefs, cooks, and comedians.

I'D KILL TO GO TO HEAVEN

For Christians, death by suicide leads to instant damnation, but an execution skirts this rule and even allows time to repent for one's sins. In eighteenth-century Sweden, Christians wishing to kill themselves would commit murder to receive a death sentence. The murderers, usually women, chose infants as their victims because they were young enough to be free of sin and did not require absolution from a priest.

THIRD TIME'S THE HARM

Described as everything from "negligent" to "a demon from hell in the disguise of a priest," Pope Benedict IX served as pope three different times between 1032 and 1048. Born into wealth, he started his first pontificate at age twenty and was outsted in 1044 for hosting particularly wild orgies. His second lasted just two months after he was caught trying to sell the papacy, and he was permanently removed from the position after a brief third term.

DECEPTION OF CHURCH AND STATE

The largest infiltration of the United States government in history was committed in the 1970s by the Church of Scientology. Operation Snow White targeted government agencies, particularly the IRS, with members stealing documents to purge any negative records about Scientology and its founder L. Ron Hubbard.

RELIGIOUS COVERT

On September 11, 1857, a wagon train headed through Utah to California was attacked by a Mormon militia. The militia had disguised themseves as members of the local Paiute tribe, but once their cover was blown, they feigned a truce and murdered 120 men, women, and children. The Mormons unsuccessfully attempted to destroy any records of the slaughter.

LET ME DRINK IT OVER

In 987 CE, Russian ruler Vladimir the Great called for a study of the world's major religions so that he could decide which would be best for his country. He immediately rejected Islam for its strict ban on alcohol consumption, and was quoted as saying: "Drinking is the joy of all Rus'. We cannot exist without that pleasure."

SIMILAR STORY ARK

The *Epic of Gilgamesh*, one of the world's oldest pieces of literature, was written in Mesopotamia (present-day Iraq and parts of other surrounding countries) sometime between 2100 and 1200 BCE. It includes a story of a man who is told to build a ship to save the world's animals from a great flood. The ship becomes lodged on a mountaintop, and birds are released to see if the waters have receeded. Two thousand years later, a very similar story would show up in the Bible.

THE LORD ON HIGH

Plants similar to those used in the psychoactive drink aya-huasca have long grown in Egypt's Sinai Peninsula, and an Israeli philosophy professor has speculated that Moses's meeting with God on Mt. Sinai was a psychedelics-induced hallucination.

HOLEY PLUMBING

In 2012, something miraculous happened in Mumbai: a statue of Jesus started crying real tears! Author Sanal Edamaruku suggested that this might actually be from a faulty sewage system (it was). He faced a major backlash from Catholics, and thanks to India's painfully vague blasphemy laws, a possible jail sentence. Edamaruku moved to Finland to evade arrest, and as of 2021 the charges have not been dropped.

HEY, BROTHER, CAN YOU SPARE A LIFE?

A Japanese man from the farming town of Shingō claimed to have discovered documents proving him to be a direct descendent of Jesus Christ. While the supposed documents were destroyed in World War II's Allied bombings, they purportedly said that Jesus had his brother take his place on the cross while he fled to Japan and lived out his life as a simple rice farmer. The town has embraced the local legend, and even has a "Tomb of Jesus" attraction.

HELL ON EARTH

Jehovah's Witnesses teach that the end times began on October 1, 1914, as that was the day the fallen angel Satan was booted from heaven and landed on Earth. For decades they preached that people alive during that year would live to see Christ's return to Earth, but some 120 years later, that doctrine has been swept under the rug.

DAMNED IF YOU DO, DAMNED IF YOU DON'T

In the late 1990s, Saddam Hussein claimed to have commissioned a copy of the Quran written with twenty-seven liters of his own blood as a gesture of thanks to God for keeping him alive for so long. While it's not clear how much (if any) real blood is in the book, Muslim leaders aren't sure what to do with it, as writing a Quran in blood is a sin, but so is destroying one.

WELL, ACTUALLY

The term *devil's advocate* originates from a former position in the Roman Catholic Church whose sole responsibility was to argue against a potential saint's beatification by finding character flaws or holes in their miracles.

MYSTERIES OF FAITH

Unicorns are mentioned in the Bible nine times.

HAMMER TIME

Vatican rites are shrouded in secrecy, but there are enduring reports of elders using a tap to the forehead with a silver hammer to confirm that a pope is actually dead and not just napping.

GOD BLESS YOU

The first Egyptian deity, Atum, was believed to have created himself from the primordial waters through sheer will. Out of loneliness, he produced children from his sneezes and spit, and some say he invented masturbation, with the hand he used representing his internal feminine side. His name, in fact, was derived from the word for "finish."

TALL ORDER

Televangelist Oral Roberts claimed that he had a vision of a nine-hundred-foot-tall Jesus commanding him to a build a hospital. City of Faith Medical and Research Center opened in 1981, and after years of hemorrhaging money, closed in 1989, $25 million in debt. The Tulsa complex is now known as City-Plex Towers and is home to a debt collection agency.

HAIL MARY

An Ohio church built a sixty-two-foot-tall statue of Jesus in 2004, which was promptly nicknamed Football Jesus due to his outstretched arms. Six years later, it was struck by lightning and burned to the ground.

WE ANSWER TO A HIGHER POWER

Members of the Native American Church can legally possess and transport the hallucinogenic drug peyote for use in religious ceremonies.

LIGHT MEAL

Breatharians claim they can exist without food or water, believing that they can glean the Hindu life force prana from sunlight. Unsurprisingly, many breatharians have died from starvation and dehydration.

PAY TO PRAY

As congregations grew, first-century priests had a hard time managing collecting the temple tax, dispensing holy water, *and* leading the flock. Mathemetician Heron of Alexandria found a solution: a sealed vase of holy water that dispensed an amount proportionate to the number of coins inserted, aka a vending machine.

MAKING THE LAW

James Oglethorpe, the founder of colonial Georgia, set up the city of Savannah (at that time the capital) around four rules, all of which were broken in short order: no booze, no lawyers, no slaves, and no Catholics. Don't worry, he wasn't discriminating against Catholics, just the Spaniards in nearby Florida.

GET ON YOUR KNEES AND PRAYS

St. Priapus Church, of the Temple of Priapus, is a pagan religion founded in the 1980s that centers around worship of the penis. Fellatio is considered the ultimate "good act."

MIRACLES ON ICE

Thomas Jefferson made his own version of the Bible. *The Jefferson Bible, or The Life and Morals of Jesus of Nazareth*, removes all supernatural acts from the ancient text.

In the thirteenth century, Pope Gregory IX issued an edict that linked cats to Satan worship. This led to open season on cat hunting, and some scholars believe that this led to an increase in disease-carrying rats, which contributed to the spread of the bubonic plague.

I'D GIVE MY LEFT AND RIGHT NUT TO BE A SINGER

Since women were supposed to remain silent in church, the Roman Catholic Church castrated prepubescent choir boys to maintain their high singing voices.

SALT LAKE SHITTY

Mormon prophet and the first governor of the Utah Territory, Brigham Young, believed that "Negroes" were the children of Cain, and their dark skin was a curse from God for the murder of Abel. Black Mormons were banned from entering the lay priesthood until 1978.

LET US PREY

Televangelist Pat Robertson founded the charity Operation Blessing to raise funds for refugees from the 1994 Rwandan genocide. Instead, he diverted funds to his African Development Corporation, a failed diamond mining company.

WE'RE NOT KIDDING

Actors Rose McGowan and Joaquin Phoenix were both born into the cult The Family International, then known as Children of God. The group preached communal living and free love, but members resigned (including the actors' families) once the leader, David Berg, began advocating for sex between children and adults.

GOD IS MY CO-PAY

Believing that help should come from the community, most Amish refuse to carry health insurance and have waived their social security benefits.

MY SOUL MY CHOICE

The Anabaptists, the branch of Christianity founded in the sixteenth century that birthed the Mennonites and Amish, believed that a person could not have salvation until they made a declaration of faith as a free-willed adult. Since this was not in alignment with official state-sanctioned Biblical interpretations, they were ruthlessly persecuted and often put to death.

BUY THE WAY

Up through the 1500s, the Catholic church allowed parishioners to purchase "indulgences," basically a "get out of hell free" card.

MAKING A NAME FOR YOURSELF

Thirteenth-century Scottish theologian Duns Scotus argued in favor of the Immaculate Conception theory of Jesus's birth, which was hotly contested at the time. While his idea caught on, later scholars found his debate tactics so insufferable that his name evolved into the modern word *dunce*.

SINNER, SINNER, CHICKEN DINNER

On the eve of Yom Kippur, some Jews practice an atonement ritual called Kapparot, in which they wave a live chicken or rooster over their heads and then slaughter it. The bird is then given to a needy family. For the squeamish, the rite can also be performed with money.

I LOVE YOU, MAN

Adelphopoiesis was an Orthodox Christian ceremony that united two people, usually men, in a bromantic union similar to siblinghood. It was practiced in the Catholic church through the fourteenth century.

CULT-LERTY

The Oneida Community was an experiment in communal living that believed in practicing free love, breeding in order to create a superior race, and that Jesus had already returned to earth in 70 CE. After thirty-three years, the community folded in 1888 and turned into the Oneida silverware company.

KIDS THESE GAYS

In 1999, televangelist and professional moron Jerry Falwell warned parents about Teletubbies, asserting that Tinky Winky was a covert gay recruitment tool due to the triangle on top of its head and snazzy red purse.

WHERE THERE'S SMOKE, THERE'S HELLFIRE

One of Christoper Columbus's explorers, Rodrigo de Jerez, was the first person to bring tobacco to Europe. At the time, the devil was the only one who could blow smoke out of his mouth, so when Rodrigo lit up in public, he was arrested, accused of being the devil, and jailed for seven years.

GOVERN-
MENTAL

AN ARMY OF PLUS-ONE

Liechtenstein's last military engagement was during the 1866 Austro-Prussian War. They sent off eighty soldiers, but returned with eighty-one as they had made an Italian friend along the way.

GIRLS MATURE FASTER

As of 2021, Iranian boys can't be held criminally responsible under the age of fifteen. But girls can be held criminally responsible starting at age nine.

GRAVE SITUATION

After running out of grave sites, the Brazilian mayor of Biritiba-Mirim filed a public bill in 2005 making it illegal for townspeople to die. If someone died, a living relative could potentially be fined or have to spend time in jail.

JUST MAROONED

In 1904, a twenty-nine-year-old Swedish sailor by the name of Carl Emil Pettersson was shipwrecked on the shores of Papua New Guinea, and was brought by the villagers to the island's king. There the king's daughter fell in love with him, married him, and he became king of the island after his wife's father died.

MICKEY DICK

Richard Nixon was at Disney World when he gave his famous "I am not a crook" speech.

OBJECT OF MY OBSESSION

After the death of Muammar el-Qaddafi in 2011, Libyan rebels found a surprising item while raiding his palace: Qaddafi's homemade scrapbook of American diplomat Condoleezza Rice.

VIRAL NEWS STORY

The KGB ran a 1980s disinformation campaign called Operation INFEKTION that pushed the idea that the United States government had developed HIV/AIDS as part of a biological weapons project. Meanwhile, Soviet scientists were reaching out to American doctors for help managing their own growing AIDS crisis.

PUT YOUR RABBIT'S FOOT IN YOUR MOUTH

Napoleon Bonaparte's brother Louis accidentally crowned himself rabbit. When he took over the Netherlands in 1806, he mispronounced "king of Holland" and instead said in broken Dutch: "I am rabbit of Holland."

WE'RE IN A JAM, BAND

After gaining independence from the USSR, Lithuania struggled economically and couldn't afford to send its basketball team to the 1992 Olympics. Fortunately for the ballers, the Grateful Dead read about their plight and sponsored their trip to the Olympics, complete with tie-dyed uniforms.

POLITICAL THEATER

In the 1970s, the tiny Polynesian nation Nauru was one of the richest in the world. Currently, they are one of the poorest, as their once-abundant natural resources were depleted and the country's chief financial adviser convinced several corrupt public officials (including the president) to invest in his failed musical about the life of Leonardo da Vinci.

NEWLY JACKED CITY

In the late nineteenth century, Chicago's city officials began work on a plan to raise the entire city four feet above Lake Michigan's water level with screw jacks. The work would take decades, but would finally provide the city with dry roads and a working sewer system. Sixteen years into the project, most of the raised buildings were lost to the Great Chicago Fire.

SCHNAPPS DECISION

In 1984, Prime Minister Robert Muldoon of New Zealand made a drunken live TV appearance, where he spontaneously called for a general election. He lost.

CAR JACKED

Hoping to establish a trade deal, Sweden sent North Korea one thousand Volvos, among other imports, in the mid '70s. North Korea never paid, and every six months Sweden sends them an invoice for the two-billion-kronor debt.

SOME VOTES CARRY MORE WEIGHT

England's 1679 Habeas Corpus Act, which gave prisoners the right to a fair trial, passed in Parliment only because its supporters jokingly counted a fat lord as ten votes; the opposition never noticed so the supporters just went with it.

THOUGHTS AND PRAYERS

The National Institutes of Health's alternative medicine branch used $666,000 in federal research money for a 1998 study to find out if prayer and psychic healing could help AIDS patients. Their findings showed that neither helped at all.

CLEAN LIVING

Amsterdam has an interesting approach to rehabilitating alcoholics: employing them as street cleaners and paying them in beer, cash, and tobacco.

HUNTING DOGS

In 1963, Haitian dictator François Duvalier, aka Papa Doc, was told that his rival had been turned into a black dog, so he very rationally responded by ordering all of the country's black dogs to be put to death.

DEVIL'S IN THE DETAILS

In 1971, Texas lawmaker Tom Moore pranked the state legislature by introducing a resolution to commend serial killer Albert DeSalvo (aka the Boston Strangler) for his "unconventional techniques involving population control." The resolution passed unanimously, and is now used as a cautionary tale about legislators not doing their homework before voting.

WHEN IN ROME

Roman Emperor Caligula's depravity
and madness were so notorious that he
is rumored to have done everything
from committing incest with his
sisters to feeding prisoners to wild
beasts to making his favorite
horse a senator.

NO SHIRT, NO SHOES,
NO SECRET SERVICE

On a 1995 US visit, Russian President Boris Yeltsin was found
by the Secret Service in front of the White house in only his
underwear, completely drunk, and trying to hail a cab so he
could go eat some pizza.

PILL SHILLS

As of 2021, New Zealand and the United States are the only
Western countries to allow pharmeceuticals to be directly advertised to consumers.

FUCK YOU MONEY

In January 2001, Saddam Hussein pledged $94 million in hu-
manitarian aid to Americans living below the poverty line.

PENCILS DOWN

In apartheid South Africa, citizens were required to register their race with the government: white, coloured (the apartheid term for mixed race), or black. Race was sometimes determined via the pencil test. If a pencil could pass through an individual's hair with ease, they were considered white. If the pencil stuck, the person was considered coloured. If a pencil was stuck and couldn't be shook out of a person's hair, they were considered black. The pencil test ended with apartheid but remains a worldwide symbol of racism.

PUB-LIC OFFICE

In Poland, there was once a political party called the Beer-Lovers' Party. It started as a prank in 1990, but they eventually came up with a serious platform and they won sixteen seats in Poland's lower house. They dissolved in 1993 shortly after they split into Large Beer and Small Beer factions.

ALMOST OUTFOXED THEM

After a successful trial run in NYC's Central Park, the US almost went ahead with Project Fantasia, a World War II psychological warfare plot involving the release of live foxes in Japan painted to mimic the kitsune, a magical creature from Japanese folklore. The project was canceled after the US found a more efficient way to wreak psychic havoc on the people of Japan: two atomic bombs.

THE KING OF KINGS

To help push their conservative moral views, Polish president Andrzej Duda and members of the clergy crowned Jesus Christ as Poland's in-name-only king.

SQUATTERS' RIGHTS

After the Cuban revolution of the 1950s, Fidel Castro attempted to cancel the US's permanent lease of the land housing the naval base and detention center at Guantánamo Bay. In 1959, the Cuban government accidentally cashed one of the US's annual rent checks, which the US still uses as proof that Cuba recognizes the lease. No checks have been cashed since.

ERR RAID

During World War II, the Japanese attached firebombs to thousands of balloons and floated them toward the western coast of the United States. Thanks to the weather, they were largely ineffective, and the sole detonation to cause casualties occurred only after the balloon was poked and prodded by the Oregon family that found it.

FASHION POLICE STATE

Because they are viewed as a symbol of American imperialism, it is illegal for North Koreans to wear blue jeans.

VIVA LA REVELATIONS

In 1975, a US military strategist working with the CIA recommended deposing Fidel Castro by spreading rumors that he was the Antichrist. The proposal went so far as to include a staged second coming, complete with pyrotechnics and a US submarine projecting an image of Jesus into the sky.

DOCTOR'S ORDERS

In eighteenth-century Denmark, the German doctor of the mentally ill King Christian VII was able to seize power for thirteen months. Before being ousted and executed, he managed to abolish slavery, torture, and censorship of the press. He even had time for an affair with the queen.

IT TAKES ONE TO KNOW ONE

In 1987, FBI agent Robert Hanssen was given an assignment: find a mole within the agency. Joke's on them, though. *He* was the mole and had been working with the KGB since 1979.

KING-SIZE BED

As a symbolic gesture of the trust between the two leaders, England's King Richard I and France's King Philip II frequently ate out of the same bowl and even slept in the same bed.

IT'S NOT FUNNY

When the Queen of England dies, the BBC will halt comedy programming for twelve days.

FLYING FIRST CLASSIFIED

There is a highly classified US airline, unofficially called Janet Airlines, that shuttles military personnel in and out of Area 51. Janet stands for "Just Another Non-Existent Terminal."

THE FUNDS DRIED UP

During World War I, Russia's Tsar Nicholas II thought banning the sale of vodka was a good wartime public health initiative, but the biggest result was the government losing a third of its annual revenue.

DON'T COME IN, I'M WRITING

Headed by the aptly named Captain Mansfield Smith-Cumming, the British intelligence agency MI6 briefly used semen as invisible ink. The agents adopted the motto "Every man his own stylo" (aka fountain pen). They stopped after realizing that despite it being invisible, the notes smelled horrible and they couldn't have their male agents masturbating every time they needed to send a note.

AN ARMY AND A LEG

After his ankle got shattered from cannon fire in 1838, Mexican general Antonio López de Santa Anna demanded his amputated leg be buried with full military honors. Six years later, he became president but was later overthrown after selling Mexican territory to the US. Enraged, the Mexican people dug up his leg and dragged it around until there was nothing left.

NAPOLEON BONE-A-SHORT

Napoleon's penis is owned by a private collector, who claims to have allowed only ten people to view the member. Those lucky enough to see it will find that the 1.5-inch member does indeed match the Emperor's modest stature.

'MERICA

NO PICNIC

The term *basket case* is rumored to be derived from World War I's quadruple amputees needing to be carried around in baskets and buggies.

WORDS TO SHIV BY

Ironically, New Hampshire license plates, featuring the state motto "Live Free or Die," are manufactured by incarcerated people.

STALLING OUT

In 2007, Idaho Republican Senator Larry Craig used the excuse that he had a "wide stance" and was picking up a piece of paper after he was arrested for soliciting sex in an airport men's room.

TALKING SOME BULLSHIT

Despite it not actually being a language, the official language in Illinois from 1923 to 1969 was "American."

SYMBOL MISUNDERSTANDING

Up until 1939, the 45th Infantry Division of the US Army featured a swastika as part of its insignia.

FRYERED UP

Because the French opposed the United States invasion of Iraq, in 2003 a Republican chairperson changed the name of French fries to "freedom fries" in the congressional cafeteria. FYI: French fries originated in Belgium, so the whole thing was even dumber that you initially thought.

DRUNKEN PREAMBLING

The signing of the Constitution came at the tail end of a two-day bender in which sixty bottles of Bordeaux, fifty-four bottles of Madeira, twenty-two bottles of porter, twelve bottles of beer, eight bottles of whiskey, eight bottles of hard cider, and seven bowls of alcoholic punch were consumed.

RIPE WITH CORRUPTION

In 1954, the United Fruit Company (now known as Chiquita) successfully lobbied the US to invade Guatemala and depose their democratically elected president because he had put a stop to brutal labor practices they relied on.

STORAGE WARS

During World War II, the US military anticipated an ongoing conflict with Japan, so they put Purple Heart production into overdrive. The surplus lasted until 1999.

POWER INTO THE PEOPLE

Under the name "The Manhattan Project," the US government detonated a nuclear bomb in New Mexico. In preparation for the 1945 event, officials tested the bomb's potential effects by intentionally exposing pregnant women and disabled children to radiation through both injections and laced oatmeal.

SEISMIC GAP

In order to protect real estate prices, the city of San Francisco intentionally underestimated the total number of deaths from a 1906 earthquake that destroyed 80 percent of the city. They reported 375 deaths when it was actually closer to three thousand.

MONUMENTAL FUCK-UP

In 2003, the US Marines built a helicopter pad on the grounds of the Hanging Gardens of Babylon in Iraq, one of the Seven Wonders of the Ancient World. The troops badly damaged the site, even filling sandbags with its crushed remnants.

OIL RIGGED

In 1953, the CIA helped overthrow the democratically elected prime minister of Iran and replace him with an authoritarian monarchy in order to control the nation's oil supply.

WASTING SPACE

In an attempt to boost morale during the Space Race, in 1958 the US concocted a super-secret plan to set off a nuclear bomb on the moon as a show of force to the Russians.

UPTIGHTY WHITIES

In 1947, the creator of Hanes underwear founded the Human Betterment League, a eugenicist organization in North Carolina whose efforts contributed to the forced sterilization of 7,600 people deemed "unworthy of having children."

GOD-DRIVEN RIGHT

Thanks to the 1973 oil crisis, Americans can turn right on red lights. Reducing the time spent idling at a light increased a car's fuel efficiency.

POSITIVE REINFORCEMENT

In World War II, the US Army had to bribe American soldiers with quarts of ice cream to keep them from killing surrendering Japanese soldiers on the spot.

IT'S A NO-BRAINER

John F. Kennedy had a sister, Rosemary, who suffered from sei-
zures and severe mood swings. At twenty-three, the family had
her lobotomized to prevent any behavior that could damage the
political future of her brothers. She was
left permanently incapacitated.

CRITTERCAL MISTAKE

After Theodore Roosevelt
popularized the Teddy
Bear, President William
Taft tried and failed to
popularize his own stuffed
animal, Billy Possum.

ON THE ROCKS

Andrew Johnson was really drunk when he took the vice presi-
dential oath of office in 1865, and went on to become the first
president to be impeached.

WASTE OF ENERGY

Jimmy Carter had thirty-two solar panels installed on the
White House in 1979, which Ronald Reagan promptly removed
after taking office.

FROM CUBAN TO CU-BANNED

The night before JFK signed the Cuban trade embargo, he placed an order for 1,200 of his favorite Cuban cigars.

SHOOK ME ALL DAY LONG

Teddy Roosevelt once held the world record for most hand-shakes in a single day with 8,150 at a White House reception.

MISSION IMPAWSIBLE

The CIA spent $20 million on an operation called Acoustic Kitty, which trained cats to spy on the Russian Embassy. It failed immediately after the first "agent" was run over by a taxi.

LAW IMBIBING CITIZENS

Nevada has a law that prohibits any county, city, or town from making public drunkenness a crime.

BATTLE OF BOWEL RUN

Dysentery, aka the Tennessee Trots, killed three times as many soldiers as combat did during the Civil War.

PRANK WAR

During Operation Mongoose, the CIA tried to assassinate Fidel Castro with exploding cigars, poisoned fountain pens, and a lethal wet suit.

GAVE THEM THE BIRD

President Andrew Jackson was notoriously profane; so much so that his pet parrot had to be removed from his funeral for swearing loudly and frequently.

REINS OF TERROR

President Franklin Pierce, the fourteenth president of the United States, was arrested after he drunkenly drove his horse carriage into an old woman in 1853.

NIECE WORK IF YOU CAN GET IT

President James Buchanan was rumored to be a "confirmed bachelor" and had his niece serve as his First Lady.

BURN AFTER READING

The CIA burns classified documents as a means to heat water at their headquarters.

HOOKERS, LINES, STINKERS

A 2015 report exposed members of the Drug Enforcement Agency for participating in "sex parties" with prostitutes hired by Colombian drug cartels.

TIMING OF HIS LIFE

President Lincoln established the Secret Service hours before his assassination.

FINDING FATHER

President Grover Cleveland took responsibility for fathering an illegitimate child during the election season of 1884 and was elected anyway.

FAILURE TO LUNCH

In 2011, the US Congress stirred up controversy when it continued to allow pizza to qualify as the vegetable requirement for school lunches.

DEFACED PROPERTY

The US government promised South Dakota's Black Hills to the Lakota Sioux in the Treaty of 1868, but the deal was promptly reneged on when gold was discovered at the base of their sacred ground in the 1870s. The 1890s brought the Battle of Wounded Knee, where countless unarmed Sioux were killed by American soldiers. It is currently the site of tourist attraction Mount Rushmore.

CIVIL WRONGS

President Lyndon B. Johnson was notorious for urinating in public, dictating notes to his aides from the toilet, and nicknaming his penis Jumbo.

VANILLA CANDIDATE

Clint Eastwood was elected mayor of Carmel-by-the-Sea, California, in 1986, after campaigning to overturn a ban on ice cream stands.

GIRLS JUST WANNA HAVE GUNS

Sarah Jane Moore and Manson Family member Lynette "Squeaky" Fromme are the only two women who have tried to assassinate a US president (Gerald Ford), and they did it within three weeks of each other.

UNDER APPRECIATED

In the 1920s, Cincinnati built an underground subway that has remained unused to this day.

BOTTOMLESS TOPLESSNESS

Portland, Oregon, is home to the world's first vegan strip club and more strip clubs per capita than anywhere else in the country.

BILL OF ALMOST RIGHTS

Thomas Jefferson proposed to prohibit slavery in all US territories in 1784, only to have his bill lose in Congress by one vote.

DON'T SHIT ON MY PARADE

President Nixon had a chemical bird repellent sprayed along his inaugural parade route to keep pigeons away, which instead left the streets littered with dead pigeons.

SECURITY BY OBSCURITY

Up until 2019, America ran its nuclear arsenal on eight-inch floppy disks. Because the technology was so outdated, it was impossible for a foreign state to hack.

SEXUAL RELEASE

In 1994, Surgeon General Joycelyn Elders was fired by Bill Clinton for saying that "Masturbation is part of human sexuality, and perhaps should be taught." This is the same Bill Clinton who abused his position as president to get a blow job from an intern.

THE RIVER STYNX

Ohio's Cuyahoga River was so polluted that it caught fire no less than thirteen times between 1868 and 1969, spurring the creation of the Environmental Protection Agency and the Clean Water Act.

STUFFING THEIR POCKETS

Thanks to some convincing from the founder of Macy's, in 1939 Franklin Delano Roosevelt moved Thanksgiving from the last Thursday to the fourth Thursday in November to increase the potential number of shopping days before Christmas.

JAZZ LETTUCE

While serving as goodwill ambassador for the US State Department in 1959, Louis Armstrong had Richard Nixon carry his trumpet case past customs because, unknown to the president, it contained three pounds of marijuana.

VOTING CAP

After the 1994 Wyoming House of Representatives race ended in a tie, the election was settled by pulling Ping-Pong balls out of a cowboy hat.

OH, MY GAUDY

You could travel all the way to Paris, France, to see the 1,063-foot Eiffel Tower, or you can go to Paris, Texas, and see a sixty-five-foot Eiffel Tower with a cowboy hat on its peak.

BORDERLINE OFFENSIVE

Operation Wetback was a 1954 immigration law enforcement program that ended up deporting several hundred legal Mexican American citizens.

PICKLING SIDES

During World War I, sauerkraut was renamed "Liberty Cabbage" as manufacturers feared no one would buy a product with a German name.

SOLVE FOR D

The *D* in D-Day stands for "day." Pretty dumb, huh?

POSTAL-TRAUMATIC STRESS DISORDER

In 1994, the Chicago arm of the US Postal Service was the subject of scandal after literal tons of undelivered mail were systematically hidden, thrown away, and burned by overwhelmed mail carriers.

WEAPON OF MASTICATION

In 2002, George W. Bush choked on a pretzel, causing him to faint and have a near-death experience.

MASTER OF YOUR DOMAIN

From 1997 to 2004, if you accidentally typed in whitehouse.com, instead of .gov, you were directed to a porn site.

PUB-LIC ACCESS

In 1656, the Massachusetts General Court passed a law requiring every town in the colony to have a pub.

MALE OPENER

During World War II, a US congressman gave President Roosevelt a bone-carved letter opener made from the arm of a dead Japanese soldier.

LAND OF THE FREE BALLS

Benjamin Franklin was an advocate of "air baths"—basically spending an hour per day reading and writing in the nude.

MILO & POTUS

John Adams was the first president to have dogs at the White House. Their names were Juno and Satan.

FAMILY TIED

Years before the whole assassination thing, Abraham Lincoln's son Robert was once saved from falling under a moving train by John Wilkes Booth's brother.

THIS LAND IS MY LAND

In 1856, the US passed a law that allows citizens to occupy any unclaimed island in the world as long as the land contains bird or bat poop, as farmers were in dire need of the nutrient-rich fertilizer.

THE FAULT IN OUR STAIRS

As of 2019, there are only two sets of escalators in the entire state of Wyoming.

VICTIM SHAMING

In 2006, Vice President Dick Cheney shot a seventy-eight-year-old acquaintance in the face while quail hunting. When he got out of the hospital, the victim apologized for any pain and suffering the vice president or his family might have experienced.

GROUNDED FOR LIFE

The Massachusetts Bay Colony passed a Stubborn Child Law in 1646 that allowed parents to put their defiant male teenagers to death. It was formally repealed in 1973.

ASSURANCE FRAUD

Operation Northwoods was a CIA plan to build support for a war against Cuba by committing genuine acts of terrorism in American cities and blaming them on Fidel Castro.

NATURE
CALLS

EWE-GE TITS

Because its DNA was derived from cells from a mammary gland, the first cloned sheep was named after busty national treasure Dolly Parton.

XXXCAVATION

A thighbone fragment from a Megalosaurus found in 1676 was originally catalogued as a Scrotum Humanum due to its resemblance to, well, a giant human scrotum.

HOOF-BAKED IDEA

In the 1930s, the Soviet Union unsuccessfully attempted to domesticate the moose for use in its cavalry.

POISON CONTROL

Possums have the ability to neutralize almost all poisons, even from creatures they have never encountered.

HEAD BUTT STUFF

Rams (male sheep) are the only animal other than humans known to engage in lifelong homosexual behavior.

HIGHBERNATING

In Russia, bears have developed an addiction to jet fuel, sniffing it to get high and then passing out.

PULL-OFF METHOD

The male argonaut octopus has a detachable penis that the female can keep with her for repeat mating.

DIGITAL ERROR

Koalas have fingerprints that are virtually indistinguishable from those of humans, sometimes creating confusion at crime scenes.

DIE-HARD FANS

After Steve Irwin died from a stingray barb, his superfans had to be reminded not to kill stingrays and cut off their tails.

SIT VICIOUS

In the nineteenth century, pit bulls were known as the Nanny Dog because of how kind and protective they were toward children.

ACCIDENTAL DISCHARGE

In 1859, British settler and avid hunter Thomas Austin brought twenty-four rabbits to Australia so he could hunt them, which lead to an infestation of ten billion rabbits by 1926.

BORN TO BE MILD

Thanks to a decades long Siberian genetic experiment in selective breeding, you can now own a floppy-eared, curly-tailed, domesticated fox for only $7,000.

TRADING FACES

In 1970, Robert J. White carried out the first successful transplant of one monkey's head to another's body. The stitched-together monkey died nine days later.

HUNGRY FOR KNOWLEDGE

In the name of science, Charles Darwin ate many of the exotic animals he encountered throughout his studies.

TUNNEL OF LOVE

Since male ducks are such aggressive maters, the females have developed a maze-like vagina full of dead ends in order to prevent fertilization from the wrong male.

NUT BUSTERS

Crows and ravens have been observed purposely dropping nuts on the street in order to have them cracked open by passing cars, saving the birds from doing the hard part themselves.

YOUR SHIT IS WEEK

Sloths are so lazy that they poop only once a week, doing a happy little poo dance when they go.

VINE DINING

Jaguars get high when they eat a vine with hallucinogenic properties called yage.

SEXUALLY REACTIVE

If you were to castrate a male frog or toad, they will turn into a reproductively functional female.

AW, HELL GNAW

In an effort to spread out the beaver population, the Idaho Department of Fish and Game airdropped the critters across the state via parachute in 1948.

STAIRWAY TO HEAVEN

Famed astronomer Tycho Brahe owned a tame elk that died after getting into some beer and drunkenly falling down his stairs.

DIS-STINKTIVE

As far as humans know, wombats are the only animal whose poop is the shape of a cube.

ANIMAL TRACKS

In order to re-create the sound of raptors barking in the film *Jurassic Park*, the movie used the sound of tortoises having sex.

MAKES DOLLARS AND SCENTS

If you ever find ambergris washed up on a beach, grab it! That whale vomit is really valuable, and it's used in a lot of perfumes.

PUPULATING THE EARTH

Puppy Pregnancy Syndrome is a mental condition where people believe that they are pregnant with puppies after being bitten by a dog.

ROOTIN' TOOTIN'

In horse shows, it was formerly common practice to insert a piece of ginger into an older horse's butt to make the animal seem younger and livelier.

TAKE A FLUID, LEAVE A FLUID

In addition to drinking their blood, vampire bats also urinate on their prey.

BAD NEWS, BEARS

Because they have a size, weight, and shape similar to an adult human, bears were first used to test out the ejector seats on a supersonic aircraft. Don't worry, the bears were only slightly injured and quickly euthanized.

FELINE FRIENDLY

Cats show you their butthole as a way of saying hello, and that they're comfortable around you. It's like their version of a handshake.

FOOD PREP

Foxes have been known to use strategically aimed pee on hedgehogs in order to get them to unroll so they can eat them.

SALTY DOGS

The common canine condition of corny-smelling feet, aka Frito Feet, is due to a bacteria found on their paws.

DOWN TO POUND

After fighting with each other, it's typical for male giraffes to engage in makeup sex.

WEB MD

One of the more unusual potential side effects of a Brazilian wandering spider bite is a four-hour erection.

SEAMS FAKE

When Europeans first came upon the platypus in 1798, they sent a sketch back home to Great Britain. Scientists initially dismissed the furry, billed, web-footed creature as a possible hoax made of several animals sewn together.

SEAFOOD MEDLEY

A lobster has its brain in its throat, its teeth in its stomach, and its kidneys in its head. It also hears with its legs and tastes with its feet.

GOING DOWN UNDER

When in captivity, female koalas have been observed engaging in lesbian orgies.

SILENT BUT DEADLY

Cougars and cheetahs are the only members of the big cat family that cannot roar and instead chirp like a bird.

CORAL REEFER

Dolphins will intentionally bite puffer fish so they can get high from the toxins they release.

DAM!

Beavers emit a delicious goo from their butts called castoreum, which is sometimes used to add vanilla flavor to foods.

DEAD IN THE WATER

In the 1980s, the Indian government came up with an unsuccessful plan to rid the Ganges River of human corpses by releasing twenty-five thousand flesh-eating turtles in its waters. The plan backfired when all the turtles were killed by poachers.

ONLY THE GOOD-LOOKING DIE YOUNG

Naked mole rats have an unusually long life span of thirty years, and they are immune to cancer.

PETTING ZOO

In eighteenth-century London, you could pay three-halfpence to get into the zoo, or you could get in for free by bringing a cat or dog to be fed to the lions.

HARD KILL TO SWALLOW

The Komodo dragon will shove a carcass down its throat by running into a tree, sometimes with so much force that it knocks the tree down.

ONE-HUMP CHUMP

After sex, male honey bees die due to their testicles exploding.

HAS, TAKES BALLS

The honey badger is regarded as the most fearless creature in the world. One tactic the honey badger employs on larger prey is to castrate them and then wait for the animal to bleed out.

DEATH PERCEPTION

When threatened, the Texas horned lizard will shoot blood from its eyes.

BONE APPETIT

Ninety percent of the bearded vulture's diet is made up of bones.

RELEASH THE BEAST

After being gifted a polar bear from the king of Norway, King Henry III let the animal live in the Tower of London on a very long leash so that it could swim and fish in the River Thames.

WILDLIFE REFUSE

Pigs used to roam freely in early-nineteenth-century New York City. They played an important role in the city's sanitation system, scavenging the filthy streets for scraps and waste to eat.

NOBLE SAVAGES

Fox tossing was a popular aristocratic blood sport in Europe during the seventeenth and eighteenth centuries. Participants would launch foxes and other animals up in the air with a sling and watch them fall.

SEA LIST CELEBRITY

The Hoff Crab is named after actor David Hasselhoff because of its hairy chest.

PAWSITIVE ID

A dog's nose print is as unique as human fingerprints and can be used for identification.

RUN AFOWL

Ever since the mid-2000s, the citizens of Brookline, Massachusetts, have been regularly terrorized and attacked by a large group of aggressive wild turkeys.

BACON ROUGE

President Teddy Roosevelt supported a bill that would have released hippopotamuses into Louisiana to eat an invasive plant and provide "lake cow bacon" to hungry Americans.

AND IT'S OFF

There was an HBO series called *Luck* that starred Dustin Hoffman. After only nine episodes, it was canceled in 2012 due to three horses having to be euthanized after on-set accidents.

MIND UNDER MATTER

The assfish not only has a terrible name, but it is also known as the vertebrate with the smallest brain-to-body weight ratio.

GOODY TWO CHEWS

The moray eel has a second set of jaws in its throat, much like the creature in the *Alien* movies.

BLUBBY CHUBBY

The blue whale has the largest penis on earth, with an average length of nine feet and a girth of thirteen inches. And that's in cold water.

THE CUTE SCIENCE

In 1894, Thomas Edison's Black Maria film studio created the original viral cat video by filming two cats boxing.

MONKEY BUSINESS

Introduced in 1938 by a tour boat operator hoping to enhance his now failed Jungle Cruise ride, approximately two hundred herpes-infected rhesus monkeys now occupy a state park in Ocala, Florida.

IT'S NOT ALL GLITZ AND GLAM-ROAR

Jackie, the MGM lion, survived a plane crash, explosion, ship-wreck, and two train wrecks while working for the company.

GONE FISSION

One of the world's largest stores of nuclear weapons is housed twenty miles outside of Seattle and is guarded by a pod of trained dolphins.

GAY FOR LAY

Gay male black swans will form a temporary throuple with a female to obtain an egg, only to shoo the female away after she lays.

DON'T SHOOT THE MESSENGER

More than 100,000 pigeons were used to send messages in World War I, with a success rate of 95 percent.

LOVE IS FOR THE BIRDS

Nikola Tesla once spent $2,000 to fix a pigeon's injuries, claiming "I loved that pigeon as a man loves a woman, and she loved me."

WHAT'S THE DOGNOSIS

In 2010, a Michigan man's pet dog saved his life by biting off his infected toe while he was passed out in a drunken stupor. The infection was caused by an undiagnosed case of Type 2 diabetes.

KEEP IT DOWN IN THERE

Mice, beavers, horses, and rabbits are all unable to vomit.

PRIMATING

Starting his work in the early 1900s, Soviet biologist Ilya Ivanovich Ivanov spent his entire life trying to create a human/chimpanzee hybrid through artificial insemination.

SEA-ZED PROPERTY

In the UK, any whale, dolphin, sturgeon, or porpoise caught near the shore immediately becomes the property of the reigning monarch.

BLOODLUST

Mosquitoes are responsible for more human deaths than any other member of the animal kingdom.

SERVICE ANIMALS

During World War II, the USA developed a weapon that would release more than a thousand bats, each attached to an incendiary bomb.

WING AND A MISS

Benjamin Franklin thought the bald eagle was a terrible symbolic animal, saying that it was "very lousy," a "rank coward," of "bad moral character," and looked like a turkey.

CAN-TANK-EROUS

Octopuses are often given puzzles in captivity to prevent them from getting bored and causing mischief like juggling hermit crabs and smashing their tanks with rocks.

DOWN WITH THE THICKNESS

The hooded seal's milk has a fat content of 60 percent and is as thick as toothpaste.

TURDHOLE POWER

Besides their mouths and noses, some turtles have the ability to breathe through their butts.

WE ONLY PECKED

Cuckold is the term for a husband whose wife is flagrantly unfaithful, and the name is derived from the cuckoo bird, who lays its eggs in other birds' nests.

FOOT SOLDIER

The horror frog is nicknamed Wolverine after the Marvel superhero because of its hair pattern and its ability to break its own bones and force them through its skin when threatened.

A REAL ANIMAL IN THE SACK

Marian Engel won a prestigious literary award in 1976 after she wrote "the most controversial novel ever written in Canada" about a lonely librarian who has sex with a bear.

IF LOOKS COULD KILL

Contrary to their super cute appearance, sea otters are known to rape and drown baby seals.

HOPPY ENDINGS

When being pursued, kangaroos will often lead the predator into a body of water and hold them underwater until they drown.

REEL TO REAL

The 2002 animated movie *Ice Age* features a saber-toothed squirrel character, a creature dreamed up by the filmmakers. Fossils of a real saber-toothed squirrel were found in Argentina in 2011.

GOOD THINGS COME IN THREES

Female wombats, kangaroos, and Tasmanian devils all have three vaginas. That's only one too many, as all male marsupials have two-pronged penises.

BUTTMUNCH

Rabbits and hares will eat their own poop in order to digest the food twice and extract as many nutrients as possible.

HURTIN' FOR A SQUIRTIN'

Male giraffes will headbutt a female in the bladder until she pees, and then taste the pee to see if she's ovulating. If she is, then it's time for giraffe sex!

LOAD BEARING

An elephant can use its penis as a fifth leg to support its weight.

QUIET ON SET

Contrary to some on-screen depictions, dinosaurs most likely lacked the vocal equipment required to roar.

DENTAL RECORD

Throughout its lifetime, an elephant will go through six sets of teeth. Once the last set is gone, the elephant will starve to death.

BIRDBRAINED

South African gamblers smoke cigarettes filled with ground-up vulture brains, a practice from traditional medicine called muti. It is said that it will give them visions of the future.

CATCHING AIR

The Western hooknose snake has a defense tactic of farting so hard that it makes a loud popping sound and sometimes lifts the snake off the ground.

NATAL ATTRACTION

Tiger shark embryos spend their entire gestational period eating each other until there's only one survivor in the womb.

LIFE OR DEATH MATER

Female ferrets can die if they don't have sex while they're in heat.

HOLED UP

Hibernating bears use a mass of dried fecal matter called tappen to block their colons while they rest. It's expelled in the spring in what must be the most satisfying poop of the year.

TENDERGROIN

A castrated reindeer makes a better working animal, as they are more docile and can grow bigger and stronger. The Sami people of Norway traditionally achieved this by biting off one of the testicles.

POOR
SPORTS

DEAD FIRST

In 1923, jockey Frank Hayes came in first place atop his horse Sweet Kiss at a Belmont Park steeplechase, despite dying from a heart attack mid-race. It was was his first and only victory, and to this day he is the only jockey to win a race while dead.

LOW-BALL OFFER

John Odom, aka Bat Man, was a minor league baseball player whose team traded him in 2008 for ten baseball bats. His new team would play the theme from *Batman* every time he was on the mound, and the constant heckling drove him to quit. Six months later he died from a heroin overdose.

BEER RUN

During 1978's inaugural Ironman Triathlon, the front-runner ran out of water and had to switch to beer, causing him to lose his lead and finish as the runner-up.

HEY, BLOTTER BLOTTER

MLB pitcher Dock Ellis threw a no-hitter in 1970. He claimed he did it while high on LSD.

CAUGHT PED-HANDED

Of all the Tour de France winners between 1961 and 2015, a whopping thirty-one of them of have either tested positive for or confessed to doping.

VERY RED CARD

Colombian soccer player Andrés Escobar accidentally scored a goal for the opposing team in the 1994 World Cup. Ten days later he was gunned down in a nightclub parking lot.

MEET YOUR HAYMAKER

Boxer Sugar Ray Robinson desperately wanted out of a 1974 match after having a nightmare in which he killed his opponent, Jimmy Doyle, in the ring. After a priest and minister convinced him to fight, Robinson delivered a fatal blow to Doyle in the sixth round.

SUPER BOWEL CHAMP

Former NFL linebacker Larry Izzo has an impressive three Super Bowl rings, but his most prized trophy is a game ball given to him by coach Bill Belichick for dropping a deuce on the sideline of an active game without anyone noticing.

OFF COURSE SHE CHEATED

At the 84th Boston Marathon in 1980, Rosie Ruiz finished with the third fastest time for any woman running a marathon, until officials learned that she barely ran any of the course. Eight days after the marathon, it was discovered that she jumped onto the course about a half mile before the finish line.

BENCHWARMERS

There is a full basketball court on the fifth floor of the United States Supreme Court Building and it's jokingly known as the Highest Court in the Land.

GOOFY STANCE

From 1978 to 1989, Norway was the only country in the world where it was illegal to buy, sell, or ride a skateboard.

IN THE ROUGH

In the middle of a 2009 night, superstar golfer Tiger Woods ran his SUV into a series of hedges and trees outside of his Florida mansion. Media attention from the crash brought his skeletons out of the closet, and it was revealed that he had had more than a dozen mistresses. Woods lost millions of dollars in endorsements, got divorced, and took a brief hiatus from golf.

WORLD CHUMPS

Despite having one of the era's highest team payrolls, the Chicago White Sox conspired with a gambling syndicate to throw the 1919 World Series in exchange for a big payout.

GOLD MEDDLING

In 2000, Spain's Paralympic basketball team won the gold. Shortly thereafter, it was revealed that ten out of the twelve team members didn't have an intellectual or physical disability.

GRIP IT AND SIP IT

In a 2017 interview, pro golf legend John Daly was asked to name his favorite beer. He replied, "I'm a Miller Lite guy, always have been, since I was eight."

EXCESSIVE CELEBRATION

Hall of Fame NFL linebacker Lawrence Taylor once arrived at a team meeting in handcuffs after spending the night with two call girls who had lost the keys.

YOU'RE OUTTA HERE

In 1979, the New York Yankees debuted a mascot named Dandy, a large pinstriped bird with a giant mustache, who just happened to resemble a former Yankee catcher Thurman Munson. A couple of weeks after Dandy's debut, Munson died in a tragic plane crash and the mustachioed mascot was immediately removed from the public eye and officially retired in 1981.

SOLED OUT

Professional Jackass and skateboarder Bam Margera had a sponsorship deal with Nike, but hated their shoes so much that he would wear other companies' shoes and slap Nike stickers on them.

THE NFL COMBINE

Due to the huge loss of players who had left the NFL to fight in World War II, the Philadelphia Eagles and Pittsburgh Steelers were forced to merge into a single team called the Phil-Pitt Steagles.

REPUTATION IS IN THE GUTTER

In the nineteenth century, bowling had nine pins and a terrible reputation, as it was played primarily in bars with a heavy culture of crime and gambling. Owning a nine-pin bowling alley was outlawed in Connecticut, so bars added a tenth pin to skirt the law. That's how we got modern-day bowling.

GIMME A R-A-I-S-E! WHAT'S THAT SPELL?!

As of 2021, the average pay for an NFL cheerleader was $150 per home game. Cheerleaders usually have to pay for their own hair, makeup, travel, and photo expenses. Compare that to the average salary of the NFL waterboy: $53,000.

AMAZING REBOUND

In 1990, Lakers star James Worthy was arrested in an undercover prostitution sting hours before a game. He went to jail, bailed himself out, and received a standing ovation from fans after arriving in the second quarter. He went on to score twenty-four points in the second half.

HEAD START

According to Mike Tyson, his first fight happened during his Brooklyn childhood after a neighborhood bully ripped the head off of his pet pigeon.

COOL YOUR JETS

In 2003, Hall of Fame quarterback Joe Namath was so drunk during a mid-game interview that he told sports reporter Suzy Kolber on live TV that he wasn't interested in talking about his former team and wanted to kiss her.

PERFORMANCE-ENHANCING CHUGS

In 1968, Swedish pentathlete Hans-Gunnar Liljenwall became the first athlete to be disqualified from the Olympics for violating anti-doping rules, after drinking two beers before his pistol shooting event to calm his nerves. The entire team was disqualified and had to return their medal.

CAREER ON ICE

In 1991, Tonya Harding became the first American female figure skater to perform a triple axel in competition. In 1994, that achievement was overshadowed when her ex-husband hired an acquaintance to hit her rival Nancy Kerrigan's knee with a club at the Olympic trials. Harding was given a lifetime ban from competing in the US.

BUN IN THE OPEN

In 2017, Serena Williams became the first tennis player to win a Grand Slam title while pregnant.

BLOW JOB

Canadian pole vaulter Shawn Barber tested positive for cocaine after winning the Canadian Olympic trials, but was allowed to compete in the 2016 Rio games after it was discovered that he accidentally ingested the cocaine by kissing a Craigslist hook-up from the night before.

CROSSOVER APPEAL

American exposition basketball team the Harlem Globetrotters claim Henry Kissinger, Pope Francis, and Nelson Mandela as honorary members.

UNDER THE TABLE

Canadian professional snooker and pool player Big Bill Werbeniuk was legendary for his drinking. In the 1970s, he was said to have drunk seventy-six cans of beer in a single game. In a 1980s match, it's rumored that after forty-two pints, his snooker/ drinking opponent passed out and Bill announced, "I'm away to the bar now for a proper drink."

LET THE FLAMES BEGIN

The relay system for carrying the Olympic torch originated during the Third Reich.

SWIGGING FOR THE FENCES

Former Red Sox player Wade Boggs is rumored to have drunk sixty-four cans of Miller Lite on a cross-country flight, and claims his personal record is 107 beers in one day.

YANKEE SWAP

In 1973, New York Yankees pitchers Fritz Peterson and Mike Kekich held separate press conferences to announce that they were swapping wives. The families had been very close, so they would be trading children and dogs as well.

WHO'S ON FIRST??

Just remember: Dick Pole, Rusty Kuntz, Johnny Dickshot, Ledell Titcomb, Pickles Dillhoefer, Pete LaCock, and Boof Bonser were all Major League Baseball players' names that reporters and announcers have had to say and write to thousands of readers and spectators.

RUNNING A MOCK

During the 2000 Summer Olympics in Sydney, a sports/comedy show created a parody mascot named Fatso the Fat-Arsed Wombat that proved to be more popular than the games' official mascot.

A FACE YOU'LL NEVER FORGET

Pro baseball player Bill Ripken had an unremarkable career, but he's best known for his 1989 trading card that went into mass circulation with the words *fuck face* written on the visible underside of his baseball bat.

CANNONBOWELS

At the opening ceremony for the 1936 Olympics, Germany released twenty-five thousand pigeons and then fired a cannon. This startled the birds, who released a deluge of pigeon poop onto the spectators.

BONESTAR STATE

At the urging of their cheer coach Suzanne Mitchell, the Dallas Cowboys Cheerleaders sued the mob-affiliated producers of the 1978 adult film *Debbie Does Dallas* for using their cheerleader uniforms in the film and damaging their brand.

THE MISTAKE ON THE LAKE

The 1974 Cleveland Indians held an ill-advised promotion: Ten Cent Beer Night. The crowd became very drunk very fast, and stormed the field. Both the Cleveland Indians and Texas Rangers had to defend themselves with bats from the Ohio fans.

SPECTER SPORT

In 2016, NBA player Metta World Peace (formerly Ron Artest) claimed he was sexually assaulted by a ghost at the notoriously haunted Skirvin Hotel in Oklahoma City.

HE SHOOTS, HE SCORES, AND SCORES, AND SCORES

Wilt Chamberlain is one of the greatest players in NBA history and holds the record for the most points scored in a single game: a hundred. He might hold another record off the court, as he's claimed to have had sex with more than twenty thousand different women.

RACE ISSUE

While Hitler did snub four-time gold medal winner Jesse Owens (along with most of the other athletes) at the 1936 Berlin Olympics, Owens remembers a bigger slight: "Hitler didn't snub me, it was FDR who snubbed me. [He] didn't even send me a telegram."

SCRUMBAGS

In 1982, members of a Pittsburgh rugby club stole human heads from a university anatomy lab and were caught playing a practice match with them.

SPITZ TAKE

At the 1972 games, nine-time Olympic champion swimmer Mark Spitz jokingly told the Russian swim team coach that his mustache increased his speed and deflected water away from his mouth. The following year every Russian male swimmer was sporting a 'stache.

RECORD-BREAKING CROWDS

During a 1979 doubleheader between the Chicago White Sox and the Detroit Tigers, the MLB held a promotion called Disco Demolition Night. Fifty thousand people showed up, many carrying vinyl disco records that were to be exploded in a crate. The explosion caused a large hole in the outfield grass, and in the ensuing chaos, thousands of fans stormed and trashed the field, which brought riot police and a second game forfeiture from the White Sox.

WHO'S RUNNING THIS THING

The 1904 Olympic marathon was a trip. The first person to cross the finish line cheated by riding in a car for eleven miles of the course. The second person to cross ingested a bunch of performance-enhancing brandy and rat poison during the race. Other contestants were chased off the course by wild dogs, choked on all the dust being kicked up, or were sidelined after eating rotten apples found along the way.

PAY TO PLAY

After the Great Depression hit Brazil, the country couldn't afford to send their athletes to the 1932 Olympics in Los Angeles. So eighty-two athletes boarded a ship and sold coffee along the way. Unfortunately, there was a $1 fee to get off the boat, and the team only had enough money to deboard sixty-seven of them, leaving fifteen athletes unable to compete.

SEXY
TIME

PROHIBI-SHIN

In 2000, Saddam Hussein banned Bermuda shorts because the exposed flesh of a man's calf might "inflame the passions of women and lead to immoral behavior."

ASTRONAUGHTY

NASA intern Thad Roberts spent seven years in federal prison after having sex with his girlfriend on top of stolen moon rocks.

SOWER POWER

Genghis Khan had so much sex (and killed so many people) that one in two hundred living males is his direct descendent.

OOZING WITH STYLE

In addition to being a chic Renaissance-era fashion statement, the codpiece also provided extra room for the bandages that were treating everyone's syphilis.

GETTING OFF COURSE

Lawrence Sperry invented the aeronautic tool "autopilot" after crashing his plane into New York Harbor while attempting to join the Mile High Club.

SAY IT, DON'T SPRAY IT

Pollution is a fourteenth-century word that originally meant the discharge of semen at any time other than during sex.

WARDROBE MALE FUNCTION

Monica Lewinsky's infamous blue dress came from the Gap, which was ruined by President Clinton after he jazzed on it with his sexaphone.

HARD SCIENCE

The boner pill Viagra was originally developed to treat cardio-vascular disease.

CRACK IT, DON'T WHACK IT

The graham cracker was invented by an American Presbyterian minister Sylvester Graham to reduce masturbation and carnal urges.

DON'T BEAT YOURSELF UP

Legendary boxer Muhammad Ali allegedly abstained from sex for two months before a big fight, claiming it made him unbeatable in the ring.

YEAST AFFECTION

Cockle bread was an aphrodisiac made by seventeenth-century English women. They would knead the dough with their butts and give it to someone they loved.

SQUEAKY WHEEL GETS MY GREASE

A mechanophile is someone who is sexually attracted to machines.

IT TAKES AN OLYMPIC VILLAGE

More than 450,000 condoms were distributed to Olympic athletes at the 2016 Rio games, more than fifty times the amount distributed at the 1988 Seoul games when the number was first tracked.

PERV'S THE WORD

The story behind the term *Peeping Tom* is that, when Lady Godiva rode through the town naked (in an effort to get her husband, the earl, to lower taxes), all of the townsfolk politely looked away except for one man named Tom.

CRACK ADDICT

Enlightenment figure Jean-Jacques Rousseau loved getting spanked so much that he would intentionally get in trouble at school, and as an adult would expose his butt in public to women in hopes of getting his hiney slapped.

MAKING IT UP

Ancient Roman philosopher Pliny the Elder posited that excessive sex would lead to your eyelashes falling out, so women took to using make up to make their eyelashes look longer as a show of chastity.

HUMP THAT RUMP

Pygophilia is the term for being sexually attracted to butts.

CLEARING ONE'S HEAD

The Japanese word *kenjataimu* (賢者タイム) means the "period after orgasm when a man is free from sexual desire and can think clearly."

WHY RISK IT

Men can reduce the risk of prostate cancer by 33 percent if they masturbate twenty-one or more times per month.

HUMMER OF '69

In 1969, oral sex was legalized in Canada.

FATAL ATTRACTION

Hybristophilia is a term for sexual attraction to someone who commits crimes.

I'M NUT FEELING SWELL

Blue balls is a real medical condition. It even has a technical term: epididymal hypertension.

GETTING HOT OFF THE PRESS

The Tale of the Two Lovers is a fifteenth-century best-selling erotic novel written by Pope Pius II.

SEXTORTION

The KGB tried to blackmail Indonesian President Achmed Sukarno with videotapes of him having sex with Russian operatives who were dressed as flight attendants. It didn't work, as Sukarno was super proud and asked for copies so he could show them off.

LOCKS OF LOVE

Created in the fifteenth century, merkins were pubic wigs that were used by prostitutes to cover their diseased genitals.

ERECT CORRELATION

Venice, Italy, still features a bridge whose name literally translates to "Bridge of the Tits," as its location was once an area where prostitutes frequently worked.

HARD-CORE FILM BUFF

One of the oldest surviving pornographic films is from 1907 and depicts three women having riverside sex with Satan.

TWO TO FOREPLAY

When it was originally created, Twister was denounced by critics as "sex in a box."

LET'S GIVE THEM A HAND

There is a volunteer organization in Taiwan called the Hand Angels. They provide hand jobs and other sexual acts for people who are disabled or unable to sexually satisfy themselves.

A SHOWER AND A KNOWER

In 2015, a group of fourteen-year-old British students invented a condom that would change color if an STI was detected.

FAMILY MATERS

Iceland has such a small population that it developed an anti-incest app to prevent accidental family hookups.

LAID OVER

Flamingo Air, a flight school and sightseeing tour company in Cincinnati, Ohio, provides flights for couples looking to join the Mile High Club.

DANCING IN THE SHEETS

David Bowie described himself as a "closet heterosexual"; according to his first wife, he had a sexual relationship with Mick Jagger.

A BODY AT REST WILL REMAIN AT REST

Isaac Newton allegedly died a virgin at the age of eighty-four.

WORKING OUT THE KINKS

Havelock Ellis, one of the first sexologists, was impotent until the age of sixty, when he realized he got aroused by the sight of a woman urinating.

TOXIC WAIST

In one Spider-Man comic series, Peter Parker's wife Mary Jane Watson died from years of exposure to his radioactive sperm.

BEAUTY IS IN THE EYE OF THE POLICYHOLDER

Esurance had to stop using their cartoon mascot, a pink-haired secret agent named Erin, after she started showing up in massive amounts of fan-made pornography. At one point, 90 percent of images in a Google search for her yielded NSFW fan-rendered results.

PLAYTHING

The Barbie doll is based on a German comic strip call girl named Lilli.

WRITIN' DIRTY

Children's author Roald Dahl wrote four adult short stories dealing with sex and other mature themes for *Playboy* in 1965.

EYE KINK, THEREFORE I AM

Noted French philosopher and mathematician René Descartes had a fetish for women with crossed eyes.

LET'S TALK ABOUT SPECTS

Spectrophilia is the sexual attraction to g-g-ghosts!

CAN BUY ME LOVE

The Beatles' song "Ticket to Ride" was inspired by Hamburg prostitutes who were given an official doctor-issued card saying that they were free of STIs.

RUNWAY BRIDE

Amelia Earhart insisted on an open marriage, including a stipulation in her 1931 prenup to not be held by "any medieval code of faithfulness."

FAPPILY EVER AFTER

Fairy tale author Hans Christian Andersen would visit brothels only to talk to the women, then masturbate at home, all while keeping a detailed diary of his jerk-off sessions.

FREE AIDVICE

Cosmopolitan magazine published an article in 1988 stating that unprotected sex with HIV-positive men was fine and didn't put women at risk.

IF IT HADN'T BEEN FOR YOU MEDDLING KIDS

In 2016, Italy's Supreme Court ruled that as long as no minors witness it, masturbating in public is not a crime.

SEXUAL ADVANCES

Ernst Gräfenberg studied the role of the woman's urethra in orgasm, developed the IUD, and has the G-Spot named after him.

SEXUAL HANG-UPS

Whoopi Goldberg once worked as a phone sex operator before becoming a star.

REVERSE THE FLOW

The word *cock*, now used for *penis*, was originally a term for *vagina*. You can hear it used with its original meaning in songs from Lil' Kim, Ice Cube, 2 Live Crew, and Snoop Dogg.

FORBIDDEN FRUIT

As of 2016, China has banned all videos of people erotically eating bananas.

SKIN IN THE GAME

In 1979, *Penthouse* magazine produced its only feature-length pornographic film, *Caligula*, starring Helen Mirren, Malcolm McDowell, and Peter O'Toole.

CLIMAXING THE CHARTS

"Love to Love You Baby" by Donna Summer became a smash hit in 1976 and features the sounds of twenty-three "orgasms."

LIKE A MOUTH TO A FLAME

During an interview with *The Guardian*, actor Michael Douglas claimed that his tongue cancer was caused by cunnilingus.

BOX ORIFICE

The 1995 stripper drama *Showgirls* was at one time the highest-grossing NC-17 rated film, despite winning seven Razzie awards including worst picture, worst actress, and worst director.

BUGGERY

Formicophilia is the term for being aroused by having insects on your genitals.

SNEAKY PEEK

In 1999, Disney recalled 3.4 million copies of the film *The Rescuers* after it was discovered that two frames contained a real photo of a naked woman in the background.

IRAQ-TICA

In 2000, Saddam Hussein wrote a best-selling romance novel called *Zabibah and the King*.

HORNY GOATEE

Due to increased testosterone production, men's facial hair will grow faster when they're anticipating sex.

MAKING A MALE ERROR

In the Middle Ages, men hoping to father a boy would have their left testicle removed because, *duh*, that's the one that girl sperm comes out of.

CAUGHT IN THE ACT

Penis captivus is the medical term for when a penis gets stuck in the vagina during intercourse.

HARD EVIDENCE

Dr. Giles Brindley once showed that the circulation drug papaverine caused erections by injecting his penis prior to a presentation and then dropping his pants and inviting the crowd to observe his boner.

BONEYARD

Mary Shelley, the author of *Frankenstein*, lost her virginity on her mother's grave.

SOMEONE DID THEIR RESEARCH

In the seventeenth century, there was a prostitution directory in the UK called *A Catalogue of Jilts, Cracks & Prostitutes, Nightwalkers, Whores, She-friends, Kind Women and other Linnen-lifting Tribe*. Here's an excerpt: Mary Holland was apparently "tall, graceful and comely, shy of her favours," but could be persuaded "at a cost of £20." Her sister Elizabeth was "indifferent to Money but a Supper and Two Guineas will tempt her."

SAW SOME ACTION

Until the 1990s, the French used to run mobile brothels to supply their frontline soldiers with prostitutes.

POLEBEARERS

In Taiwan, strippers are sometimes hired to dance at funerals as a way to attract mourners, distract evil spirits, and give the deceased an extra-rowdy send-off.

BIRTH COINTREAU

People have been trying to avoid having babies for as long as people have been making babies. In ancient China, women drank lead and mercury. During the Middle Ages in Europe, women were advised to wear the testicles of a weasel on their thighs or hang its amputated foot around their necks. In sixteenth-century Canada, women drank a contraceptive potion made from moonshine and dried beaver testicles.

BEDDING CRASHERS

In eighteenth-century Europe, it wasn't uncommon for select guests at a royal wedding to escort the bride and groom into the bedding ceremony and witness the consummation.

SIGHT FOR SORE EYES

There is a strain of chlamydia called trachoma that turns your eyelashes inward, causing them to scratch your eyes every time you blink and can even lead to blindness.

LABOR DAY

Certain regions in Russia celebrate Day of Conception on September 12. People are given the day off to do it and make babies. Women who give birth exactly nine months later are given cars, refrigerators, and other fantastic prizes!

TASTELESS

TURN FOR THE WURST

For much of the 2010s, Volkswagen produced more currywurst sausages than they did automobiles. The sausages are served mainly in their factory cafeterias, and are also available at some supermarkets and football stadiums.

WE DON'T HAVE COKE, IS FANTA OKAY?

Because of a 1941 US trade embrago, the German division of Coca-Cola created Fanta as a Coke substitute since they couldn't get the necessary ingredients to make Coca-Cola.

WHERE'S THE BEEF?

In 2013, a scandal struck European grocery stores when it was found that ground beef and other beef products contained up to 100 percent horse meat.

FOOD INSPECTOR

Even though they eventually acquired the rights to use him in their marketing, Popeyes was not named for the cartoon sailor. Founder Al Copeland said that Jimmy "Popeye" Doyle, the dogged NYPD detective played by Gene Hackman in the 1971 movie *The French Connection*, was the original inspiration for the name.

ONE OUT OF TEN DENTISTS APPROVE

In a truly impressive act of synergy, cotton candy was invented in the late 1800s by dentist William Morrison with an assist from a candymaker. They debuted the treat at the St. Louis World's Fair, where a box of their "Fairy Floss" cost almost twice as much as admission to the event.

ICE CREAM SOCIAL

Prior to his brief tenure as Trump's White House press secretary, Sean Spicer instigated a years-long one-sided Twitter war with novelty ice cream company Dippin' Dots.

PARTY IN THE PANTRY

Vanilla extract has no age restrictions to purchase despite the fact that it is required by the FDA to have a minimum alcohol content of 35 percent.

FAMILY RECIPE

People indigenous to the Columbia River Valley were known to prepare a special cured acorn dish renamed Chinook Olives by European settlers. Here's the recipe: 1. Dig a hole near the entrance of your shelter. 2. Fill that pit with thirty-five liters of acorns. 3. Cover the acorns with a thin layer of grass and half a foot of dirt. 4. For the next six months, make everyone in your family pee on your acorn pit. 5. Dig them up and enjoy!

SPOOKY DOOKIE

There was a brief scare in the 1970s when children were being admitted to the ER with what appeared to be internal bleeding. In fact, it was the red dyes in Franken Berry cereal that had caused their pink poo. The official name of the condition is Franken Berry Stool.

CHECKS OUT

Probably due to their supernatural shelf life, a hurricane in the forecast will make strawberry Pop-Tarts surpass beer as Walmart's top-selling product.

TASTES HEAVENLY

Pets de Soeur is a French pastry whose name translates to "nun farts."

MORE LIKE RADI-YUM!

Advertised as "a cure for the living dead," Radithor was an old-timey energy drink produced by a New Jersey radium lab in the 1920s. It was indeed radioactive, but thanks to the ridiculously high price, only a small amount of consumers lost their jaws to radium poisoning.

THE SCRAPPIEST PLACE ON EARTH

To fund his theme park passion project, Walt Disney crammed as many brand sponsors as he could into the original Disneyland. Fritos (now Frito-Lay) was one of them, with their Casa de Fritos restaurant. This became the birthplace of the Dorito, as the managers needed a way to monetize their leftover tortilla scraps.

DROP IT LIKE IT'S HOT

Grandiosa frozen pizza is so popular in Norway that when the company released the jingle "Respect for Grandiosa," it reached number one on the Norwegian pop charts and stayed there for eight weeks.

BOTTOMFEEDERS

In colonial America, eating a lobster was the equivalent to eating a rat and they were regularly served to prisoners.

I AIN'T NO FRUIT

Despite the fact that they're considered a fruit almost everywhere else, Oklahoma's official state vegetable is the watermelon.

STARVING FOR ATTENTION

Michel Lotito was a French entertainer from the 1960s and '70s who had pica, a psychological disorder characterized by an appetite for non-food items. He would eat things like bicycles, shopping carts, televisions, and a Cessna plane, which took him two years to finish.

LOSING YOUR LUNCH

The barf used in the original *Exorcist* film was made out of canned pea soup.

SNACK ATTACK

Hammond Pretzel Company is a family-owned bakery that has operated for decades in Lancaster, Pennsylvania. Their cult following extended to the White House, where they were a favorite of a young Chelsea Clinton. A Hammond pretzel would go on to cause George W. Bush's infamous choking incident.

MY WEINER RULES

According to the National Hot Dog and Sausage Council, it is unacceptable for anyone over the age of eighteen to put ketchup on a hot dog. Mustard, relish, onions, cheese, and chili are acceptable.

FOOD FIGHT

In 2006, a US court of law ruled that burritos are not a sandwich after a Panera Bread sued their shopping center for renting a space to a Qdoba Mexican Grill. Panera believed that the shopping center breached a clause in their lease that prevented them from renting space to other sandwich shops.

DON'T EAT YOUR GREENS

Before kale's 2010s renaissance, Pizza Hut was America's biggest buyer of the leafy green. It wasn't even served to customers, but instead used to decorate their salad bars.

ATTACK ON THE KILLER TOMATOES

Between the years 1500 and 1800, European settlers in America avoided tomatoes, as they were believed to be poisonous and sinful due to their rumored aphrodiasic properties. That all ended in 1820 when a man named Robert Johnson, who had enjoyed the fruit abroad, stood before a Salem, New Jersey, crowd and ate a whole basket of tomatoes without dying.

PIE IN THE SKY

In 2001, Pizza Hut paid the Russian space agency $1 million to send a pizza to the International Space Station. The Americans present weren't allowed to partake in the pie, as NASA has strict rules against brands advertising on their spacecrafts.

POP CULTURE

Caffeine-heavy soda Mountain Dew gets its name from an old-timey slang term for moonshine, which is fitting because it was originally crafted as a mixer for whiskey.

NO RIGHT WAY TO EAT A WHOPPER

On April 1, 1998, Burger King introduced a Left-Handed Whopper with all the condiments rotated 180 degrees. It attracted thousands of customers who didn't realize it was an April Fools' prank.

ONCE YOU DROP, YOU CAN STOP

Fredric Baur, the inventor who designed the iconic Pringles can, was so proud of his creation that he requested to have some of his ashes buried in an Original flavor Pringles can.

BIPOLAR DISODA

There used to be a soft drink called "Bib-Label Lithiated Lemon-Lime Soda" which contained the mood-stabilizing drug lithium citrate, still used to treat bipolar disorders today. In 1948, they ditched the drugs and rebranded it as 7 Up, named after lithium's atomic mass.

PULLING IT FOR THE KIDS

In 2012, Kit Kat pulled its bear-suited mascot after Twitter pointed out its similarity to a pedophilia-related meme called Pedobear.

GLUTTONY FOR PUNISHMENT

Sin eating is a ritual practiced around the world, where eating food symbolizes the spiritual transfering of sins from the deceased to the living. For instance, in Bavaria, a piece of food is placed on the chest of the deceased and then eaten by the nearest relative.

MANIFEAST DESTINY

Thanks to selective breeding to meet consumer demand, the average weight of a turkey in the US has gone from twelve pounds in 1920 to more than thirty pounds today.

STEALTHY EATING

Before she was a culinary icon, Julia Child cooked up a repellent recipe for the US during World War II to prevent curious sharks from setting off explosives targeted at German U-boats.

WHAT THE FLOCK

A small bird called an ortolan is the star of a bizarre French dish, prepared by force feeding it grain, drowning it in brandy, and setting it to roast, to be consumed whole (bones and all) while the diner wears a towel on top of their head. The towel is said to hide the shamefully decadent act from God.

PRAYING FOR A PAYOUT

A man attempted to sue Applebee's after he was burned while praying over a sizzling skillet of fajitas. His lawsuit was dismissed, as a trial judge found that the restaurant was not required to warn the man against obvious dangers.

SOUP TO NUTS

There is a soup in Filipino cuisine known as Soup Number Five. Rumored to have aphrodesiac properties, the soup contains all parts of a bull's sex organs.

MORE SPOONING, LESS FORKING

Kellogg's Corn Flakes were invented by a sanitarium director who believed that a bland diet would help reduce masturbation and sexual energy.

SMOKED EGGPLANT

Eggplant seeds have a little bit of nicotine in them. You'd have to eat twenty eggplants to get the same buzz you'd get from one cigarette.

ACKNOWLEDGMENTS

Sh*t for Brains wouldn't be here without the early involvement of two very important people: Matt Russell and Cole Cooney. They are two of the funniest and smartest people we know, and each brought different and invaluable perspectives to both the content and structure of this project. Best of all, they never, EVER let our friendship get in the way of telling us when our jokes suck.

Thank you to Reed's Local, a Chicago neighborhood bar, for giving us the time and space to workshop our stuff with a weekly live trivia night. If you see us there, this round's on you!

Thank you to our agent, Jason Yarn, for helping us navigate this new territory; to Marian Lizzi at Penguin for plucking us out of obscurity and lighting the fuse on our skyrocket to fame (we assume that's what happens next); and to our editor, Lauren Appleton, for being the ultimate good sport with the most insightful pair of fresh eyes we could hope for.

Thank you in advance to whichever bottom-tier streaming service turns *Sh*t for Brains* into a game show.

And, most important, thank you to the friends and family who picked up the slack at home, indulged every "wait, I need to look something up real quick," suffered through some pretty brutal first drafts of our (now flawless, thankyouverymuch) puns, and provided countless smiles and nods for every "dude, guess what I just read!" We are truly humbled by the volume of support you've provided. We will never be able to repay you, so we won't embarrass ourselves by trying.

ABOUT THE AUTHOR

Harebrained is a Chicago-based trio dedicated to all things awesome. They share an appreciation for pop culture deep cuts, their dogs and cats, design, and regional sandwiches. Two of them are visual artists by trade and native Midwesterners; one of them is good at typing stuff and would prefer you not know her point of origin. Briefly internet famous for creating "Period Panties," their line of ridiculous women's underwear, they have been working together for years and friends for even longer.